SIR WILLIAM TEMPLE

Observations
upon the United Provinces
of the Netherlands

SIR WILLIAM TEMPLE

Observations upon the United Provinces of
the Netherlands

With an Introduction by

G. N. CLARK

*Chichele Professor of Economic History
in the University of Oxford*

CAMBRIDGE
AT THE UNIVERSITY PRESS
1932

CAMBRIDGE UNIVERSITY PRESS
Cambridge, New York, Melbourne, Madrid, Cape Town,
Singapore, São Paulo, Delhi, Tokyo, Mexico City

Cambridge University Press
The Edinburgh Building, Cambridge CB2 8RU, UK

Published in the United States of America by
Cambridge University Press, New York

www.cambridge.org
Information on this title: www.cambridge.org/9781107698451

First published 1932
First paperback edition 2011

A catalogue record for this publication is available from the British Library

ISBN 978-1-107-69845-1 Paperback

CONTENTS

Introduction   *page* vii

Preface   xi

Chapter I Of the Rise and Progress of the
             United Provinces   1

        II Of their Government   56

       III Of their Scituation   89

        IV Of their People and Dispositions   97

         V Of their Religion   116

        VI Of their Trade   128

       VII Of their Forces and Revenues   151

      VIII The Causes of their Fall in 1672   158

INTRODUCTION

In the letters about his travels which were published in 1687 the historian Gilbert Burnet referred to Sir William Temple's *Observations upon the United Provinces* as 'the most perfect book of its kind that is perhaps in being' and we learn from a contemporary letter that this caused it to be 'bought up mightily upon a suddaine.' It was already in its fourth edition, and it had held for fourteen years the position of the leading English authority on the Dutch republic, better in expression and arrangement and judgment than any of the numerous other books on that state, and as well-informed as any of them. When Temple published it in 1673 the Dutch and the English were at war for the third time within his recollection, and he seems to have written it for the occasion, though a remark in the Preface suggests that parts of it (especially perhaps the second chapter) were copied or adapted from a formal report after his embassy, which ended in 1670 when the war was brewing. The experience of this and his other visits to Holland, from his first private visit in 1652, were the main sources of the book. He refers in it to some historical writers, but not by name to contemporary political or economic authors. Nor, in the later editions, did he make any attempt to bring it up to date. He seems only to have corrected it once: I believe this was for the second edition, but, as this is not in the British Museum or the Bodleian, I have not seen these alterations in any edition earlier than the third. They are not important. The brief account of the provinces other than Holland at the end of chapter II is an addition; the paragraph about the Zuyder Zee is lengthened; and in chapter V the words 'and not admitted to any publick charges' are added to the account of the Roman Catholics. That is all, and the subsequent editions contribute nothing except changes in spelling and capitals and some new printer's errors. The present reprint follows the text of the fifth edition published in 1690. No alterations have been made except that obvious misprints have been corrected.

Temple was characteristically pleased with his book. He wrote that he wished King Charles II had leisure to read his two short chapters on religion and trade. As time went on he must have seen himself that the book was not perfect. Before very long it was pointed out that he had shown the reasons of the fall of the United Provinces 'before they were down.' A generation later the cosmopolitan reviewer Jean le Clerc examined it minutely. He drew attention to some minor obscurities in the constitutional part, to the needlessly guarded statements about the soundness of the Bank of Amsterdam, to the error of describing the prosperous years 1669 and 1670 as a time when Dutch foreign trade was bad, and to the too-close identification of the states-party with Arminianism. Beyond that he could find no errors of fact except that the water in the Haarlemmer Meer was not fresh but brackish. It is indeed not in errors but in omissions that a modern reader finds the book weakest. There is nothing about Dutch painting or learning or science, three of the great wonders of that age. And if Temple had known anything about Dutch poetry he would not have made his absurd remarks about the Dutch as lovers.

His purpose in writing was not merely to convey information about the Dutch, but to explain and indeed to expatiate. He gives his views not only on politics, and economics and history, but on geology and human character and medicine. As specimens of the thought of his time they are all interesting and some of them are important. His passage about the spleen may border on the irrelevant, but it belongs to the same point of view with what he has to say about the low rate of interest and trade cycles and (not wisely) about population or the balance of trade. What holds the book together is a method of interpreting history, a method which is summed up in the dictum: 'Most national customs are the effect of some unseen, or unobserved, natural causes or necessities.' This idea and ideas related to it were kindling much of the best thought of that time, and Temple must have been in contact with them from his youth. As an undergraduate at Cambridge his humour was too lively to pursue the harsh studies of logic and philosophy and he spent most of his time on 'entertainments,' especially tennis; but, even so, two years at Emmanuel with Cudworth as his tutor may have taught him much without his knowing it.

Since the book is explanatory it requires little explanation even now. For the few rare or obsolete words, including the Gallicisms (*licensed, fond, force, digues*), it is not necessary to look further than the *Oxford English Dictionary*. Some of the place-names are oddly spelt, but they are not difficult except perhaps 'the Burse' or 'the Barse,' variants of 'the Buss,' the then familiar English name for 'den Bosch' or Bois-le-Duc. I wish I knew exactly how Temple came to pitch on the village of Molkwerum near Stavoren as a type of the old Germanic settlement: the paragraph in which he talks about it anticipates modern historical methods in a most striking way. There are indeed plenty of other passages which illustrate the scantiness and inaccuracy of the historical information at Temple's disposal; but, although in the seventeenth century modern historical methods were only beginning to be used, their emergence was a vital part of a great intellectual movement. Knowledge from every branch of science was being brought to bear on the interpretation of human history and human society, and the permanence of this book is due to Temple's belief in this study as one science among the others.

G. N. CLARK

OXFORD
24 *October* 1932

PREFACE

Having *lately seen the State of the* United Provinces, *after a prodigious growth in Riches, Beauty, extent of Commerce, and number of Inhabitants, arrived at length to such a height, (by the strength of their Navies, their fortified Towns, and standing-Forces, with a constant Revenue, proportion'd to the support of all this Greatness,) as made them the Envy of some, the Fear of others, and the Wonder of all their Neighbours.*

We have, this Summer past, beheld the same State, in the midst of great appearing Safety, Order, Strength, and Vigor, almost ruin'd and broken to pieces, in some few days, and by very few blows; And reduced in a manner to its first Principles of Weakness, and Distress; exposed, opprest, and very near at Mercy. Their Inland Provinces swallowed up by an Invasion, almost as sudden, and unresisted, as the Inundations to which the others are subject. And the remainders of their State rather kept alive by neglect, or disconcert of its Enemies, than by any strength of Nature, or Endeavours at its own recovery.

Now, because such a Greatness and such a Fall of this State seem Revolutions unparallel'd in any Story, and hardly conceived, even by those who have lately seen them; I thought it might be worth an idle Man's time, to give some account of the Rise and Progress of this Commonwealth, The Causes of their Greatness, And the steps towards their Fall: Which were all made by motions, perhaps, little taken notice of by common Eyes, and almost undiscernible to any Man, that was not placed to the best advantage, and something concerned, as well as much enclin'd, to observe them.

The usual Duty of employments abroad, imposed not only by Custom, but by Orders of State, made it fit for me to prepare some formal Account of this Country and Government, after Two years Ambassy, in the midst of great Conjunctures and Negotiations among them. And such a Revolution as has since happen'd there, though it may have made these Discourses little important to His Majesty, or His Council; Yet it will not have render'd them less agreeable to common Eyes, who, like Men that live near the Sea, will run out upon the Cliffs to gaze at it in a Storm, though they would not look out of their Windows, to see it in a Calm.

Besides, at a time when the Actions of this Scene take up, so generally, the Eyes and Discourses of their Neighbours; And the Maps of their Country grow so much in request: I thought a Map of their State and Government would not be unwelcome to the World, since it is full as necessary as the others, to under-stand the late Revolutions, and Changes among them. And as no Man's Story can be well written till he is dead; so the account of this State could not be well given till its fall, which may justly be Dated from the Events of last Summer, (what-ever Fortunes may further attend them,) since therein we have seen the sudden and violent dissolution of that more Popular Government, which had continued, and made so much noise, for above Twenty Years in the World, without the exercise, or in-fluence, of the Authority of the Princes of Orange, a Part so Essential in the first Constitutions of their State. Nor can I wholly lose my pains in this Adventure, when I shall gain the ease of answering this way, at once, those many Questions I have lately been used to, upon this occasion: Which made me first observe, and wonder, how ignorant we were, generally, in the Affairs and Constitutions of a Country, so much in our Eye, the common road of our Travels, as well as subject of our

Talk; and which we have been of late, not only curious, but concerned, to know.

I am very sensible, how ill a Trade it is to write, where much is ventur'd, and little can be gain'd; since, whoever does it ill is sure of contempt; and the justliest that can be, when no Man provokes him to discover his own follies, or to trouble the World, if he writes well, he raises the envy of those Wits that are possest of the Vogue, and are jealous of their Preferment there, as if it were in Love, or in State; And have found, that the nearest way to their own Reputation lies, right or wrong, by the derision of other Men. But, however, I am not in pain, for 'tis the affectation of Praise, that makes the fear of Reproach; And I write without other design than of entertaining very idle Men, and, among them, my self. For I must confess, that being wholly useless to the Publique; And unacquainted with the Cares of encreasing Riches, (which busie the World:) Being grown cold to the pleasures of younger or livelier Men; And having ended the Entertainments of Building, and Planting, (which use to succeed them;) finding little taste in common Conversation, and trouble in much Reading, from the care of my Eyes (since an illness contracted by many unnecessary diligences in my Employments abroad;) there can hardly be found an idler Man, than I; Nor consequently, one more excuseable for giving way to such amusements, as this: Having nothing to do, but to enjoy the ease of a private Life and Fortune; which, as I know no Man envies, so (I thank God,) no Man can reproach.

I am not ignorant, that the vein of Reading never ran lower than in this Age; and seldom goes further than the design of raising a Stock to furnish some Calling, or Conversation. The Desire of Knowledge being either laught out of doors by the Wit, that pleases the Age; or beaten out by Interest, that so

much possesses it: And the amusement of Books giving way to
the liberties or refinements of Pleasure, that were formerly less
known, or less avowed, than now. Yet some there will always
be found in the World, who ask no more at their idle hours,
than to forget themselves. And, whether that be brought about
by Drink or Play, by Love or Business, or by some diversions,
as idle as this, 'tis all a case.

Besides, it may possibly fall out, at one time or other, that
some Prince, or great Minister, may not be ill pleased in these
kind of Memorials, (upon such a Subject,) to trace the steps of
Trade and Riches, of Order and Power in a State; and those
likewise of weak or violent Counsels; of corrupt, or ill, Con-
duct; of Faction or Obstinacy, which decay and dissolve the
firmest Governments: That so, by Reflections upon Foreign
Events, they may provide the better and the earlier against
those at home, and raise their own Honour and Happiness, by
equal degrees with the Prosperity and Safety of the Nations,
they Govern.

For, under favour of those who would pass for Wits in our
Age, by saying things, which David *tells us, the Fool said in*
His; And set up with bringing those Wares to Market, which
(God knows) have been always in the World, though kept up in
corners, because they used to mark their Owners, in former
Ages, with the Names of Buffoons, Prophane, *or* Impudent,
Men; *Who deride all Form and Order, as well as Piety and*
Truth; And, under the notion of Fopperies, endeavour to
dissolve the very Bonds of all Civil Society; though by the
Favour and Protection thereof, they themselves enjoy so much
greater proportions of Wealth, and of Pleasures, than would
fall to their share, if all lay in common, as they seem to design,
(for then such Possessions would belong of right to the strongest
and bravest among us.)

Under favour of such Men, I believe, it will be found, at one time or other, by all who shall try, That whilst Human Nature continues what it is, The same Orders in State, The same Discipline in Armies, The same Reverence for things Sacred, And Respect of Civil Institutions, The same Virtues and Dispositions of Princes and Magistrates, derived by Interest, or Imitation, into the Customs and Humors of the People, will ever have the same Effects upon the Strength and Greatness of all Governments, and upon the Honour and Authority of those that Rule, as well as the Happiness and Safety of those that Obey.

Nor are we to think Princes themselves losers, or less entertain'd, when we see them employ their Time, and their Thoughts, in so useful Speculations, and to so Glorious Ends: But that rather, thereby they attain their true Prerogative of being Happier, as well as Greater, than Subjects can be. For all the Pleasures of Sense, that any Man can enjoy, are within the reach of a private Fortune, and ordinary Contrivance; Grow fainter with Age, and duller with use; Must be revived with intermissions, and wait upon the returns of Appetite, which are no more at call of the Rich, than the Poor. The flashes of Wit and good Humour, that rise from the Vapours of Wine, are little different from those that proceed from the heats of Blood in the first approaches of Fevers, or Frenzies; And are to be valued, but as (indeed) they are, the effects of Distemper. But the pleasures of Imagination, as they heighten and refine the very pleasures of Sense, so they are of larger extent, and longer duration. And if the most sensual Man will confess there is a Pleasure in Pleasing, He must likewise allow, there is Good to a Man's Self, in doing Good to others; And the further this extends, the higher it rises, and the longer it lasts. Besides, there is Beauty in Order; and there

are Charms in well-deserved Praise: And both are the greater,
by how much greater the Subject; As the first appearing in a
well-framed and well-governed State; And the other arising
from Noble and Generous Actions. Nor can any veins of good
Humour be greater than those, that swell by the success of wise
Counsels, and by the fortunate Events of publique Affairs;
since a Man that takes pleasure in doing good to Ten thousand,
must needs have more, than he that takes none, but in doing
Good to Himself.

    But these Thoughts lead me too far, and to little purpose:
Therefore I shall leave them for those I had first in my Head,
concerning the State of the United-Provinces.

    And whereas the Greatness of their Strength, and Revenues,
grew out of the vastness of their Trade, into which, their
Religion, their Manners, and Dispositions, their Scituation,
and the Form of their Government, were the chief Ingredients.
And this last had been raised partly upon an old Foundation,
And partly with Materials brought together, by many and
various Accidents; It will be necessary for the Survey of this
great Frame, to give some account of the Rise and Progress of
their State, by pointing out the most remarkable Occasions of
the first, and Periods of the other. To discover the Nature and
Constitutions of their Government in its several parts, and the
motions of it, from the first and smallest Wheels. To observe,
what is peculiar to them in their Scituation, or Dispositions,
And what in their Religion. To take a Survey of their Trade,
and the Causes of it; Of the Forces and Revenues, which com-
posed their Greatness; And the Circumstances, and Con-
junctures, which conspired to their Fall. And these are the
Heads, that shall make the Order and Arguments in the
several parts of these Observations.

Of the Rise and Progress of the United Provinces

Whoever will take a view of the Rise of this Commonwealth, must trace it up as high as the first Commotions in the *Seventeen Provinces*, under the Duchess of *Parma's* Government; and the true Causes of that more avowed and general Revolt in the Duke of *Alva's* time. And, to find out the natural Springs of those Revolutions, must reflect upon that sort of Government under which the Inhabitants of those Provinces lived for so many Ages past, in the subjection of their several Dukes or Counts; till by Marriages, Successions or Conquest, they came to be united in the House of *Burgundy*, under *Philip* sirnamed *The Good*: And afterwards in that of *Austria*, under *Philip* Father of *Charles* in the Person of that great Emperor incorporated with those vast Dominions of *Germany* and *Spain*, *Italy* and the *Indies*.

Nor will it be from the purpose upon this search, to run a little higher into the Antiquities of these Countries: For though most Men are contented only to see a River as it runs by them, and talk of the changes in it, as they happen; when 'tis troubled, or when clear; when it drowns the Country in a Flood, or forsakes it in a Drowth: Yet he, that would know the nature of the Water, and the Causes of those Accidents (so as to guess at their continuance or return), must find out its source, and observe with what strength it rises, what length it runs, and how many small streams fall in, and feed it to such a height, as make it either delightful or terrible to the Eye, and useful or dangerous to the Country about it.

The Numbers and Fury of the Northern Nations, under many different names, having by several Inundations broken down the whole frame of the *Roman* Empire, extended in their Provinces as far as the *Rhine*; either gave a birth, or made way for the several Kingdoms and Principalities, that have since continued in the parts of *Europe* on this side that River, which made the ancient Limits of the *Gallick* and *German* Nations. The Tract of Land, which we usually call the *Low-Countries*, was so wasted by the Invasions or Marches of this raging People, (who past by them to greater Conquests,) that the Inhabitants grew thin; and being secure of nothing they possest, fell to seek the support of their Lives, rather by hunting, or by violence, than by Labour and Industry; and thereby the grounds came to be uncultivated, and in the course of years turned either to Forrest, or Marshes; which are the two natural Soils of all desolated Lands in the more temperate Regions. For by soaking of frequent show'rs, and the course of Waters from the higher into lower Grounds, when there is no issue that helps them to break out into a Channel, the flat Land grows to be a mixture of Earth and Water, and neither of common use nor passage to Man or Beast, which is call'd a Marsh. The higher, and so the drier, parts, moistned by the Rain, and warm'd by the Sun, shoot forth some sorts of Plants, as naturally as Bodies do some sort of Hair; which, being preserved by the desolateness of a place untrodden, as well as untill'd, grow to such Trees or Shrubs as are natural to the Soil, and those in time producing both Food and Shelter for several kind of Beasts, make the sort of Country we call a *Forest.*

And such was *Flanders* for many years before *Charlemaign's* time, when the Power of the *Francs*, having raised and establisht a great Kingdom of their own, upon the entire Conquest of *Gaul*, began to reduce the disorders of that Country to the form of a Civil, or (at least) Military Government; To make divisions and distributions of Lands and Jurisdictions, by the Bounty of the Prince, or the Services of his chief Followers and Commanders; To one of whom, a great extent of this Land was given, with the Title of *Forester of Flanders*. This Office continued for several descents, and began to civilize the Country, by repressing the violence of Robbers and Spoilers, who infested the Woody and Fast-places, and by encouraging the milder People to fall into Civil Societies, to trust to their Industry for subsistence, to Laws for protection, and to their Arms united under the Care and Conduct of their Governours, for Safety and Defence.

In the time of *Charlemaigne*, as some write; or, as others, in that of *Charles the Bald*, *Flanders* was erected into a County, which changed the Title of *Forester* for that of *Count*, without interrupting the Succession.

What the extent of this County was at first, or how far the Jurisdiction of *Foresters* reached, I cannot affirm; nor whether it only bordered upon, or included, the lower parts of the vast Woods of *Ardenne*, which in *Charlemaigns's* time, was all Forest as high as *Aix*, and the rough Country for some Leagues beyond it, and was used commonly by that Emperor for his Hunting: This appears by the ancient Records of that City, which attribute the discovery, or at least, retrieving the knowledge of those hot Baths, to the fortune of that Prince, while he was Hunting: For his Horse poching one of his Legs into some hollow ground, made way for the smoaking water to break out, and gave occasion for the Emperor's building that City, and making it his usual Seat, and the place of Coronation for the follow-ing Emperors.

Holland, being an Island made by the dividing-branches of the ancient *Rhyne*, and called formerly *Batavia*, was esteemed rather a part of *Germany* than *Gaul*, (between which it was seated,) in regard of its being planted by the *Catti*, a great and ancient People of *Germany*, and was treated by the *Romans* rather as an Allied than Subjected Province; who drew from thence no other Tribute besides Bands of Soldiers, much esteemed for their Valour, and joyned as Auxiliaries to their Legions in their *Gallick*, *German*, and *Brittish* Wars.

'Tis probable, this Island changed in a great measure Inhabitants and Customs, as well as Names, upon the in-roads of the barbarous Nations, but chiefly of the *Normans* and *Danes*, from whose Countries and Language the Names of *Holland* and *Zealand* seem to be derived. But about the Year 860. a Son of the Count of *Frize*, by a Daughter of the Emperor *Lewis* the Second, was by him instituted Count of *Holland*, and gave beginning to that Title; which, running since that time through so many direct or collateral Successions and some Usurpations, came to an end at last in *Philip* the Second, King of *Spain*, by the defection of the *United Provinces*.

Under these first *Foresters* and *Counts*, who began to take those wasted Countries and mixed People into their Care, and to intend the growth, strength, and riches of their Subjects, which they esteemed to be their own; Many old and demolisht Castles were re-built, many new ones erected, and given by the Princes to those of their Subjects or Friends whom they most loved or esteemed, with large circuits of Lands for their support, and Seigneurial Jurisdiction over the Inhabitants. And this upon several easie Conditions, but chiefly of attendance on their Prince at the necessary times of either honouring him in Peace, or serving him in War. Nay possibly, some of these Seigneuries and their Jurisdictions, may, as they pretend, have been the remains of some old Principalities in those Countries among the *Gallick* and *German* Nations, the first Institutions whereof were lost in the immensity of time that preceded the *Roman* Discoveries or Conquest, and might be derived perhaps from the first Paternal Dominion, or Concurrence of loose People into orderly Neighborhoods, with a deference, if not subjection, to the wisest or bravest among them.

Under the same Counts were either founded or restored many Cities and Towns; of which the old had their ancient Freedoms and Jurisdictions confirmed, or others annexed; and the New had either the same granted to them by example of the others; or great Immunities and Priviledges for the encouragement of Inhabitants to come and People in them: All these Constitutions agreeing much in substance perhaps by imitation, or else by the agreeing nature of the People, for whom, or by whom, they were framed; but differing in form according to the difference of their Original, or the several Natures, Customs and Interests of the Princes, whose Concessions many of them were, and all their Permissions.

Another Constitution which entred deep into their Government, may be derived from another source. For those Northern Nations whose unknown Language and Countries perhaps made them be called *Barbarous*, (though indeed almost all Nations out of *Italy* and *Greece* were styled so by the *Romans*,) but whose Victories in obtaining new Seats, and Orders in possessing them, might make us allow them for a better policy'd People, than they appeared by the vastness of their multitude, or the rage of their Battels.

Wherever they past, and seated their Colonies and Dominions, they left a Constitution which has since been called in most *European* Languages, *The States*; consisting of Three Orders, *Noble*, *Ecclesiastical*, and *Popular*, under the limited Principality of one Person, with the style of *King*, *Prince*, *Duke*, or *Count*. The remainders at least, or traces hereof, appear still in all the Principalities founded by those People in *Italy*, *France* and *Spain*; and were of a piece with the present Constitutions in most of the great Dominions on t'other side the *Rhyne*: And it seems to have been a temper first introduced by them between the Tyranny of the Eastern Kingdoms, and the Liberty of the *Grecian* or *Roman* Commonwealths.

'Tis true, the *Goths* were Gentiles when they first broke into the *Roman* Empire, till one great swarm of this People, upon Treaty with one of the *Roman* Emperors, and upon Concessions of a great Tract of Land to be a Seat for their Nation, embraced at once the Christian Faith. After which, the same People breaking out of the Limits had been allowed them, and by fresh numbers bearing all down where they bent their march; as they were a great means of propagating Religion in many parts of *Europe* where they extended their Conquests; so the Zeal of these new Proselytes, warmed by the veneration they had for their Bishops and Pastors, and enriched by the spoils and possessions of so vast Countries, seem to have been the First that introduced

the maintenance of the Churches and Clergy, by endow-
ments of Lands, Lordships, and Vassals, appropriated to
them: For before this time the Authority of the Priesthood
in all Religions seemed wholly to consist in the Peoples
Opinion of their Piety, Learning, or Virtues, or a Reverence
for their Character and Mystical Ceremonies and Institutions; their Support, or their Revenues, in the voluntary
Oblations of pious Men, the Bounty of Princes, or in a
certain share out of the Labours and Gains of those who
lived under their Cure, and not in any subjection of Mens
Lives or Fortunes, which belonged wholly to the Civil
Power: And *Ammianus*, though he taxes the Luxury of
the Bishops in *Valentinian's* time, yet he speaks of their
Riches which occasioned or fomented it, as arising wholly
from the Oblations of the People. But the Devotion of
these new Christians introducing this new form of en-
dowing their Churches; and afterwards *Pepin* and *Charlemaign* King of the *Franks*, upon their Victories in *Italy*, and
the favour of the *Roman* Bishop to their Title and Arms,
having annexed great Territories and Jurisdictions to that
See: This Example, or Custom, was followed by most
Princes of the Northern Races through the rest of *Europe*,
and brought into the Clergy great possessions of Lands,
and by a necessary consequence a great share of a Temporal
Power, from the dependances of their Subjects or Tenants;
by which means they came to be generally one of the three
Orders that composed the Assembly of the States in every
Country.

This Constitution of the States had been establisht from
time immemorial in the several Provinces of the *Low-
Countries*, and was often assembled for determining Disputes
about succession of their Princes, where doubtful or

contested; For deciding those between the great Towns:
For raising a Milice for the defence of their Countries in the
Wars of their Neighbors; For Advice in time of Dangers
abroad, or Discontents at home; But always upon the new
Succession of a Prince, and upon any new Impositions that
were necessary on the People. The use of this Assembly was
another of those Liberties, whereof the Inhabitants of these
Provinces were so fond and so tenacious. The rest, besides
those antient Priviledges already mentioned of their
Towns, were Concessions and Graces of several Princes, in
particular Exemptions or Immunities, Jurisdiction both in
choice and exercise of Magistracy and Civil Judicature
within themselves; or else in the customs of using none but
Natives in Charges and Offices, and passing all weighty
Affairs by the great Council composed of the great Lords
of the Country, who were in a manner all Temporal, there
being but three Bishops in all the Seventeen Provinces, till
the time of *Philip* the Second of *Spain*.

The Revenues of these Princes consisted in their ancient
Demesnes, in small Customs, (which yet grew considerable
by the greatness of Trade in the Maritime Towns,) and in
the voluntary Contributions of their Subjects, either in the
States, or in particular Cities, according to the necessities of
their Prince, or the affections of the People. Nor were these
frequent; for the Forces of these Counts were composed of
such Lords, who either by their Governments, or other
Offices; or by the tenure of their Lands, were obliged to
attend their Prince on Horseback, with certain numbers of
Men, upon all his Wars: or else of a Milice, which was call'd
Les gens d'ordonnance, who served on foot, and were not
unlike our Train-bands; the use, or at least style whereof,
was renewed in *Flanders* upon the last War with *France* in

1667, when the Count *Egmont* was made by the Governor, General *de gens d'ordonnance*.

These Forces were defrayed by the Cities or Countries, as the others were raised by the Lords when occasion required; and all were licensed immediately when it was past, so that they were of little charge to the Prince. His Wars were but with other Princes of his own size, or Competitors to his Principality; or sometimes with the Mutinies of his great Towns; Short, though Violent; and decided by one Battle or Siege; unless they fell into the quarrels between *England* and *France*, and then they were engaged but in the skirts of the War, the gross of it being waged between the two Kings, and these smaller Princes made use of for the credit of Alliance, or sometimes the commodiousness of a Diversion, rather than for any great weight they made in the main of the Affair.

The most frequent Wars of the Counts of *Holland*, were with the *Frisons*, a part of the old *Saxons*; and the fiercest battels of some of the Counts of *Flanders*, were with the *Normans*, who past that way into *France*, and were the last of those Nations that have infested the more Southern parts of *Europe*. I have somtimes thought, how it should have come to pass, that the infinite swarm of that vast Northern-Hive, which so often shook the World like a great Tempest, and overflowed it like a Torrent; changing Names, and Customs, and Government, and Language, and the very face of Nature, wherever they seated themselves; which, upon record of story, under the name of *Gauls*, pierced into *Greece* and *Italy*, sacking *Rome*, and besieging the Capitol in *Camillus* his time; under that of the *Cimbers*, marcht through *France*, to the very confines of *Italy*, defended by *Marius*; under that of *Huns* or *Lombards*, *Visigoths*, *Goths*, and *Vandals*, conquered the whole Forces of the *Roman* Empire, sackt *Rome* thrice in a small compass of years; seated three Kingdoms in *Spain* and *Africk*, as well as *Lombardy*; and under that of *Danes* or *Normans*, possest themselves of *England*, a great part of *France*, and even of *Naples* and *Sicily*. How (I say) these Nations, which seemed to spawn in every Age, and at some intervals of time discharged their own native Countries of so vast Numbers, and with such terror to the World, should about seven or eight hundred years ago leave off the use of these furious Expeditions, as if on a sudden they should have grown barren, or tame, or better contented with their own ill Climates. But I suppose, we owe this benefit wholly to the growth and progress of Christianity in the North; by which, early and undistinguisht Copulation, or multitude of Wives, were either restrained or abrogated; By the same means Learning and Civility got footing among them in some degree, and enclosed certain Circuits of those vast Regions, by the distinctions and bounds of Kingdoms, Principalities, or Commonalties. Men began to leave their wilder lives, spent without other Cares or Pleasures, than of Food, or of Lust; and betook themselves to the ease and entertainment of Societies: With Order and Labour, Riches began, and Trade followed; and these made way for Luxury, and that for many Diseases or ill habits of Body, which, unknown to the former and simpler Ages, began to shorten and weaken both Life and Procreation. Besides, the divisions and circles of Dominion occasioned Wars between the several Nations, though of one Faith; and those of the *Poles*, *Hungarians*, and *Muscovites*, with the *Turks* or *Tartars*, made greater slaughters; and by these Accidents I suppose the Numbers of those fertil Broods have been lessened, and their Limits in a measure confined; and we have had thereby, for so long together in these parts of the World, the Honour and Liberty of Drawing our own Blood, upon the quarrels of Humor or Avarice, Ambition or Pride, without the assistance, or need, of any barbarous Nations to destroy us.

But to end this digression, and return to the *Low-Countries*, where the Government lasted, in the form and manner described, (though in several Principalities,) till *Philip* of *Burgundy*, in whom all the Seventeen Provinces came to be united.

By this great extent of a populous Country, and the mighty growth of Trade in *Bruges*, *Gant*, and *Antwerp*, attributed by *Comines* to the goodness of the Princes, and ease and safety of the People; both *Philip*, and his Son *Charles the Hardy*, found themselves a Match for *France*, then much weakened, as well by the late Wars of *England*, as the Factions of their Princes. And in the Wars with *France*, was the House of *Burgundy*, under *Charles* and *Maximilian* of *Austria*, (who Married his Daughter and Heir) and afterwards under *Charles* the Fifth, their Grandchild, almost constantly engaged; the course, successes, and revolutions whereof are commonly known.

Philip of *Burgundy*, who began them, was a good and wise Prince, lov'd by his Subjects, and esteemed by his Enemies; and took his measures so well, that, upon the declining of the *English* Greatness abroad, by their Dissentions at home, he ended his quarrels in *France*, by a Peace, with Safety and Honour. So that he took no pretence from his Greatness, or his Wars, to change any thing in the Forms of his Government: But *Charles the Hardy* engaged more rashly against *France*, and the *Switzers*, began to ask greater and frequent Contributions of his Subjects; which, gain'd at first by the credit of his Father's Government and his own great Designs, but spent in an unfortunate War, made his People discontented, and him diseesteemed, till he ended an unhappy Life, by an untimely Death, in the Battel of *Nancy*.

In the time of *Maximilian*, several *German* Troops were brought down into *Flanders* for their defence against *France*; and in that of *Charles* the Fifth, much greater Forces of *Spaniards* and *Italians*, upon the same occasion; a thing unknown to the *Low-country-men* in the time of their former Princes. But through the whole course of this Emperor's Reign, who was commonly on the fortunate hand, his Greatness and Fame encreasing together, either diverted or suppressed any discontents of his Subjects upon the increase of their Payments, or the grievance of so many Foreign Troops among them. Besides, *Charles* was of a gentle and a generous Nature; and, being born in the *Low-Countries*, was naturally kind and easie to that People, whose Customs and Language he always used when he was among them, and employed all their great Men in the Charges of his Court, his Government, or his Armies, through the several parts of his vast Dominions; so that upon the last great Action of his life, which was the resignation of his Crowns to his Son and Brother, he left to *Philip* the Second, the Seventeen Provinces, in a condition as Peaceable, and as Loyal, as either Prince or Subjects could desire.

Philip the Second, coming to the possession of so many and great Dominions, about the year 1556, after some trial of good and ill fortune in the War with *France*, (which was left him by his Father, like an encumbrance upon a great

Estate,) restored, by the Peace of *Cambrey*, not only the quiet of his own Countries, but in a manner of all Christendom, which was in some degree or other engaged in the quarrel of these Princes. After this, he resolved to return into *Spain*, and leave the *Low-Countries* under a subordinate Government, which had been till *Charles* the Fifths time the constant Seat of their Princes, and shar'd the Presence of that great Emperor with the rest of his Dominions. But *Philip*, a *Spaniard* born, retaining, from the Climate or Education of that Country, the Severeness and Gravity of the Nation, which the *Flemings* called Reservedness and Pride; Conferring the Offices of his House, and the Honour of his Council and Confidence, upon *Spaniards*, and thereby introducing their Customs, Habits, and Language into the Court of *Flanders*: Continuing, after the Peace, those *Spanish* and *Italian* Forces, and the demand of Supplies from the States which the War had made necessary, and the easier supported; He soon left off being lov'd, and began to be feared by the Inhabitants of those Provinces.

But *Philip* the Second thought it not agreeing with the Pomp and Greatness of the House of *Austria*, already at the head of so mighty Dominions; nor with his Designs of an yet greater Empire, to consider the Discontents or Grievances of so small a Country; nor to be limited by their ancient Forms of Government: And therefore, at his departure for *Spain*, and substitution of his natural Sister the Dutchess of *Parma*, for Governess of the *Low-Countries*, assisted by the Ministry of *Granvell*, he left her instructed to continue the Foreign Troops, and the demand of Money from the States for their support, which was now by a long course of War grown customary among them, and the Sums only disputed between the Prince and the States: To

establish the Fourteen Bishops, he had agreed with the
Pope, should be added to the Three, that were anciently in
the *Low-Countries*: To revive the Edicts of *Charles* the
Fifth against *Luther*, publish't in a Diet of the Empire about
the year 1550, but eluded in the *Low-Countries* even in that
Emperor's time; and thereby to make way for the Inquisition with the same course it had received in *Spain*; of
which the *Lutherans* here, and the *Moors* there, were made
an equal pretence. And these points, as they came to be
owned and executed, made the first Commotions of Mens
Minds in the Provinces.

The hatred of the People against the *Spaniards*, and the
Insolencies of those Troops, with the charge of their
support, made them look't upon by the Inhabitants in
general, as the Instruments of their Oppression and Slavery,
and not of their Defence, when a general Peace had left
them no Enemies: And therefore the States began here their
Complaints, with a general Consent and Passion of all the
Nobles, as well as Towns and Country. And upon the
delays that were contrived, or fell in, the States first refused
to raise any more Monies either for the *Spaniards* Pay, or
their own standing Troops; and the people ran into so great
despair, that in *Zealand* they absolutely gave over the
working at their Digues, suffering the Sea to gain every
Tide upon the Country; and resolving (as they said) rather
to be devoured by that Element, than by the *Spanish*
Soldiers: So that after many Disputes and Intrigues between
the Governess and the Provinces, the King, upon her
Remonstrances, was induced to their removal; which was
accordingly performed with great joy and applause of the
People.

The erecting of Fourteen new Bishops Sees, raised the

next Contest. The great Lords lookt upon this Innovation as a lessening of their Power, by introducing so many new Men into the great Council. The Abbats (out of whose Lands they were to be endowed) pleaded against it, as a violent usurpation upon the Rights of the Church, and the Will of the Dead, who had given those Lands to a particular use. The Commons murmured at it, as a new degree of Oppression upon their Conscience or Liberty, by the erecting so many new Spiritual Courts of Judicature, and so great a number of Judges, being Seventeen for Three, that were before in the Country; and those depending absolutely upon the Pope, or the King. And all Men declaimed against it, as a breach of the King's Oath at his accession to the Government, for the preserving the Church and the Laws in the same state he found them. However, this Point was gain'd entirely by the Governess, and carried over the head of all opposition, though not without leaving a general discontent.

In the midst of these ill Humors stirring in *Flanders*, the Wars of Religion, breaking out in *France*, drove great numbers of *Calvinists* into all those parts of the *Low Countries* that confine upon *France*, as the Troubles of *Germany* had before of *Lutherans*, into the *Provinces* about the *Rhine*; and the Persecutions under Queen *Mary*, those of the Church of *England* into *Flanders* and *Brabant*, by the great commerce of this Kingdom with *Bruges* and *Antwerp*.

These Accidents and Neighborhoods filled these Countries, in a small tract of Time, with swarms of the Reformed Professors: And the Admiration of their Zeal, the Opinion of their Doctrine and Piety, the Compassion of their Sufferings, the Infusion of their Discontents, or the Humour of the Age, gain'd them every day many Proselytes in the *Low-Countries,* some among the Nobles, many among the Villages, but most among the Cities, whose Trade and Riches were much encreased by these new Inhabitants; and whose Interest thereby, as well as Conversation, drew them on to their Favour.

This made work for the *Inquisition,* though moderately exercised by the Prudence and Temper of the Governess, mediating between the rigor of *Granvell,* who strained up to the highest his Master's Authority, and the execution of his Commands, upon all occasions; and the resoluteness of the Lords of the Provinces, to temper the King's Edicts, and protect the Liberties of their Country against the admission of this New and Arbitrary Judicature, unknown to all ancient Laws and Customs of the Country; and for that, not less odious to the People, than for the cruelty of their executions. For, before the *Inquisition,* the care of Religion was in the Bishops; and before that, in the Civil Magistrates throughout the Provinces.

Upon angry Debates in Council, but chiefly upon the universal Ministry of *Granvell,* a *Burgundian* of mean Birth, grown at last to a Cardinal; and more famous for the greatness of his Parts, than the goodness of his Life. The chief Lords of the Country (among whom the Prince of *Orange,* Counts *Egmont* and *Horn,* the Marquess of *Berghen* and *Montigny,* were most considerable) grew to so violent and implacable an hatred of the Cardinal, (whether from Passion or Interest,) which was so universally spread through the whole Body of the People, either by the Causes of it, or the Example, that the Lords first refused their attendance in Council, protesting, *Not to endure the sight of a Man so absolute there, and to the ruin of their Country*: And afterwards petitioned the King in the name of the whole Country,

for his removal: Upon the delay whereof and the continuance of the Inquisition, the People appeared, upon daily
occasions and accidents, heated to that degree, as threatned
a general Combustion in the whole Body, when ever the
least Flame should break out in any part.

But the King at length consented to *Granvell's* recess, by
the Opinion of the Dutchess of *Parma*, as well as the persuit
of the Provinces: Wherupon the Lords reassumed their
places in Council; Count *Egmont* was sent into *Spain* to
represent the Grievances of the Provinces; and being
favourably dispatcht by the King, especially by remitting the
rigor of the Edicts about Religion, and the Inquisition, all
noise of Discontent and Tumult was appeased, the Lords
were made use of by the Governess in the Council, and
Conduct of Affairs; and the Governess was by the Lords
both Obeyed and Honoured.

In the beginning of the Year 1565. there was a Conference
at *Bayonne* between *Katherine* Queen-Mother of *France* and
her Son *Charles* the Ninth, (though very young,) with his
Sister *Isabella* Queen of *Spain*: In which no other person
but the Duke of *Alva* interven'd, being deputed thither by
Philip, who excused his own Presence, and thereby made
this Enterview pass for an effect or expression of kindness
between the Mother and her Children. Whether great
Resolutions are the more suspected, where great Secresie is
observed; or it be true, what the Prince of *Orange* affirmed to
have by accident discovered, That the extirpation of all
Families which should profess the New Religion in the
French or *Spanish* Dominions, was here agreed on, with
mutual assistance of the two Crowns; 'Tis certain, and was
owned, that Matters of Religion were the subject of that
Conference; and that soon after, in the same Year, came

Letters from King *Philip* to the Dutchess of *Parma*, dis-
claiming the Interpretation which had been given to his
Letters by Count *Egmont*; declaring, His Pleasure was,
That all Hereticks should be put to death without remission:
That the Emperor's Edicts, and the Council of *Trent*,
should be published and observed; and commanding, That
the utmost assistance of the Civil Power should be given to
the *Inquisition*.

When this was divulged, at first, the astonishment was
great throughout their Provinces; but that soon gave way to
their Rage, which began to appear in their Looks, in their
Speeches, their bold Meetings and Libels; and was encreased by the miserable spectacles of so many Executions
upon account of Religion. The Constancy of the Sufferers,
and Compassion of the Beholders, conspiring generally to
lessen the opinion of Guilt or Crime, and heighten a
detestation of the Punishment and desire of Revenge,
against the Authors of that Counsel, of whom the Duke
of *Alva* was esteemed the Chief.

In the beginning of the Year, 1566. began an open
Mutiny of the Citizens in many Towns, hindring Executions, and forcing Prisons and Officers; and this was
followed by a Confederacy of the Lords, Never to suffer
the *Inquisition* in the *Low-Countries*, as contrary to all Laws,
both Sacred and Prophane, and exceeding the Cruelty of
all former Tyrannies. Upon which, all resolutions of
Force or Rigor grew unsafe for the Government, now too
weak for such a revolution of the People; and on the other
side, *Brederode*, in confidence of the general Favour, came
in the head of Two hundred Gentlemen, thorow the Provinces, to *Brussels*, and in bold terms petitioned the Governess for abolishing the *Inquisition*, and Edicts about

Religion; and that new ones should be fram'd by a Convention of the States.

The Governess was forced to use gentle Remedies to so violent a Disease; to receive the Petition without shew of the resentment she had at heart, and to promise a representation of their Desires to the King; which was accordingly done: But though the King was startled with such consequences of his last Commands, and at length induced to recall them; yet, whether by the slowness of his Nature, or the forms of the *Spanish* Court, the Answer came too late: And as all his former Concessions, either by delay, or testimonies of ill-will or meaning in them, had lost the good Grace; so this lost absolutely the Effect, and came into the *Low-Countries* when all was in flame, by an insurrection of the meaner people through many great Towns of *Flanders*, *Holland*, and *Utrecht*; who fell violently upon the spoil of Churches, and destruction of Images, with a thousand circumstances of barbarous and brutish Fury; which, with the Institution of Consistories and Magistrates in each Town among those of the Reformed Profession, with Publick Confederacies and Distinctions, and private Contributions agreed upon for the support of their common Cause, gave the first date in this year of 1566. to the revolt of the *Low-Countries*.

But the Nobility of the Country, and the richest of the People in the Cities, though unsatisfied with the Government, yet feeling the Effects, and abhorring the Rage, of popular Tumults, as the worst mischief that can befall any State; And encouraged by the arrival of the King's Concessions, began to unite their Councils and Forces with those of the Governess, and to employ themselves both with great Vigor and Loyalty, for suppressing the late

Insurrections, that had seized upon many, and shaked most of the Cities of the Provinces; in which the Prince of *Orange* and Count *Egmont* were great Instruments, by the Authority of their great Charges, (One being Governor of *Holland* and *Zealand*, and the other of *Flanders*;) but more by the general love and confidence of the People; Till by the reducing *Valenciens*, *Maestricht*, and the *Burse*, by Arms; The submission of *Antwerp* and other Towns; The defection of Count *Egmont* from the Councils of the Confederate Lords (as they were called;) The retreat of the Prince of *Orange* into *Germany*; and the death of *Brederode*, with the news and preparations of King *Philip's* sudden journy into the *Low-Countries*, as well as the Prudence and Moderation of the Dutchess, in governing all these circumstances; The whole Estate of the Provinces was perfectly restored to its former Peace, Obedience, and, at least, Appearance of Loyalty.

King *Philip*, whether having never really decreed his journy into *Flanders*, or diverted by the pacification of the Provinces, and apprehension of the *Moors* rebelling in *Spain*, or a distrust of his Son Prince *Charles* his violent Passions and Dispositions, or the expectation of what had been resolved at *Bayonne*, growing ripe for execution in *France*, gave over the discourse of seeing the *Low-Countries*; But at the same time took up the resolution for dispatching the Duke of *Alva* thither at the head of an Army of Ten thousand Veterane *Spanish*, and *Italian*, Troops, for the assistance of the Governess, the execution of the Laws, the suppressing and punishment of all, who had been Authors or Fomenters of the late Seditions.

This Result was put suddenly in execution, though wholly against the Advice of the Dutchess of *Parma* in

Flanders, and the Duke of *Ferin* (one of the Chief Ministers) in *Spain*: Who thought, the present Peace of the Provinces ought not to be invaded by new occasions; nor the Royal Authority lessened, by being made a Party in a War upon his Subjects; nor a Minister employed, where he was so professedly both hating, and hated, as the Duke of *Alva* in the *Low-Countries*.

But the King was unmoveable; so that in the end of the Year 1567, the Duke of *Alva* arrived there with an Army of Ten thousand, the best *Spanish* and *Italian* Soldiers, under the Command of the choicest Officers, which the Wars of *Charles* the Fifth, or *Philip* the Second, had bred up in *Europe*; which, with Two thousand *Germans* the Dutchess of *Parma* had raised in the last Tumults, and under the Command of so Old and Renowned a General as the Duke of *Alva*, made up a Force, which nothing in the *Low-Countries* could look in the face with other Eyes, than of Astonishment, Submission, or Despair.

Upon the first report of this Expedition, the Trading People of the Towns and Country began in vast Numbers to retire out of the Provinces; so as the Dutchess wrote to the King, That, in few days, above a Hundred thousand Men had left the Country, and withdrawn both their Money and Goods, and more were following every day: So great Antipathy there ever appears between Merchants and Soldiers; whilst one pretends to be safe under Laws, which the other pretends shall be subject to his Sword, and his Will. And upon the first Action of the Duke of *Alva* after his arrival, which was the seizing Count *Egmont* and *Horn*, as well as the suspected death of the Marquess of *Berghen*, and imprisonment of *Montigny* in *Spain*, (whither, some Months before, they had been sent with Commission and Instructions from the Dutchess,) she immediately desired leave of the King to retire out of the *Low-Countries*.

This was easily obtained, and the Duke of *Alva* invested in the Government, with Powers never given before to any Governour: A Council of Twelve was erected for Tryal of all Crimes committed against the King's Authority, which was called by the People, *The Council of Blood*. Great numbers were condemned and executed by Sentence of this Council, upon account of the late Insurrections; More by that of the *Inquisition*, against the parting-advice of the Dutchess of *Parma*, and the Exclamations of the People at those illegal Courts. The Towns stomached the breach of their Charters, the People of their Liberties, the Knights of the Golden-Fleece the Charters of their Order, by these new and odious Courts of Judicature; All complain of the disuse of the States, of the introduction of Armies, but all in vain: The King was constant to what he had determined; *Alva* was in his nature cruel and inexorable; the new Army was fierce and brave, and desirous of nothing so much as a Rebellion in the Country; The People were enraged, but awed and unheaded; All was Seizure and Process, Confiscation and Imprisonment, Blood and Horror, Insolence and Dejection, Punishments executed, and meditated Revenge: The smaller Branches were lopt off apace; the great ones were longer a hewing down. Count *Egmont* and *Horne* lasted several Months; but, at length, in spight of all their Services to *Charles* the Fifth, and to *Philip*; as well of their new Merits, in the quieting of the Provinces, and of so great Supplications and Intercessions as were made in their Favour, both in *Spain* and in *Flanders*, they were publickly beheaded at *Brussels*, which seemed to break all patience in the People; and, by their end, to give those commotions a beginning, which cost *Europe* so much Blood, and *Spain* a great part of the *Low-Country*-Provinces.

After the Process of *Egmont* and *Horne*, the Prince of *Orange*, who was retired into *Germany*, was summoned to his Trial for the same Crimes, of which the others had been accused; and, upon his not appearing, was condemned, proclaimed Traitor, and his whole Estate, which was very great in the Provinces, (and in *Burgundy*) seized upon, as forfeited to the King. The Prince, treated in this manner while he was quiet and unarmed in *Germany*, employs all his Credit with those Princes engaged to him by Alliance, or by common fears of the House of *Austria*, throws off all Obedience to the Duke of *Alva*, raises Forces, joyns with great numbers flocking to him out of the Provinces; All enraged at the Duke of *Alva's* Cruel and Arbitrary Government, and resolved to revenge the Count *Egmont's* death, (who had ever been the Darling of the People.) With these Troops he enters *Friesland*, and invades the outward parts of *Brabant*, receives succors from the Protestants of *France*, then in Arms under the Prince of *Conde*: And after many various Encounters and Successes, by the great Conduct of *Alva*, and Valour of his Veterane Army, being hindred from seizing upon any Town in *Brabant*, (which both of them knew would shake the Fidelity of the Provinces,) he is at length forced to break up his Army, and to retire into *Germany*. Hereupon, *Alva* returns in Triumph to *Brussels*; and, as if he had made a Conquest, instead of a Defence, causes out of the Cannon taken from *Lewis* of *Nassau*, his Statue to be cast in Brass, treading and insulting upon two smaller Statues, that represented the Two Estates of the *Low-Countries*; And this to be erected in the Cittadel he had built at *Antwerp*, for the absolute subjecting of that rich, populous, and mutinous Town.

Nothing had raised greater indignation among the *Flemings*, than the publique sight and ostentation of this Statue; and the more, because they knew the boast to be true, finding their ancient Liberties and Priviledges (the Inheritance of so many Ages, or Bounty of so many Princes) all now prostrate before this one Man's Sword and Will, who from the time of *Charles* the Fifth had ever been esteemed an Enemy of their Nation, and Author of all the Counsels for the absolute subduing their Country.

But *Alva*, mov'd with no Rumors, terrify'd with no Threats from a broken and unarmed People, and thinking no Measures nor Forms were any more necessary to be observed in the *Low-Countries*, pretends greater sums are necessary for the pay and reward of his Victorious Troops, than were annually granted upon the King's Request, by the States of the Provinces: And therefore demands a general Tax of the Hundredth part of every Man's Estate in the *Low-Countries*, to be raised at once: And for the future, the Twentieth of all Immoveables, and the Tenth of all that was Sold.

The States, with much reluctancy, consent to the first, as a thing that ended at once; but refused the other two, alledging the poverty of the Provinces, and the ruin of Trade. Upon the Duke's persisting, they petition the King by Messengers into *Spain*, but without redress; draw out the Year in Contests, sometimes stomachful, sometimes humble, with the Governor; Till the Duke, impatient of further delay, causes the Edict, without consent of the States, to be published at *Brussels*. The People refuse to pay, the Soldiers begin to levy by force; the Townsmen all shut up their Shops; the People in the Country forbear the Market, so as not so much as Bread or Meat is to be bought in the Town. The Duke is enraged, and calls the Soldiers to arms, and commands several of the Inhabitants, who refused the payments, to be hanged that very night upon their Sign-posts; which nothing moves the Obstinacy of the People. And now the Officers and the Guards are ready to begin the Executions, when news comes to Town of the taking of the *Briel* by the *Gueses*, and of the expectation That had given of a sudden Revolt in the Province of *Holland*.

This unexpected blow struck the Duke of *Alva*; and foreseeing the consequences of it, because he knew the Stubble was dry, and now he found the Fire was fallen in, he thought it an ill time to make an end of the Tragedy in *Brabant*, whilst a new Scene was opened in *Holland*; and so, giving over for the present his Taxes and Executions, applies his Thoughts to the suppression of this new Enemy, that broke in upon him from the Sea; and for that reason, the bottom and reach of the Design, as well as the nature and strength of their Forces, were to the Duke the less known, and the more suspected. Now because this seizure of the *Briel* began the second great Commotion of the *Low-Countries* in 1570, and that which indeed never ended, but in the loss of those Provinces, where the death of the *Spanish* and Royal Government gave life to a new Commonwealth; It will be necessary to know, what sort of Men, and by what Accidents united, and by what Fears or Hopes emboldned, were the first Authors of this Adventure.

Upon *Brederode's* delivering a Petition to the Dutchess of *Parma*, against the *Inquisition*, and for some liberty in point of Religion; Those Persons, which attended him, looking mean in their Cloaths and their Garb, were called by one of the Courtiers at their entrance into the Palace, *Gueses*, which signifies *Beggars*; a Name, though raised by chance or by scorn, yet affected by the Party, as an expression of Humility and Distress, and used ever after by both sides, as a Name of distinction, comprehending all, who dissented from the *Roman* Church, how different soever in Opinion among themselves.

These Men, spread in great numbers through the whole extent of the Provinces, by the accidents and dispositions, already mentioned, after the appeasing of their first Sedition, were broken in their common Counsels; and by the Cruelty of the Inquisition, and Rigor of *Alva*, were in great multitudes forced to retire out of the Provinces, at least, such as had means or hopes of subsisting abroad: Many of the poorer and more desperate fled into the Woods of the upper Countries, (where they are thick and wild,) and liv'd upon spoil; and, in the first descent of the Prince of *Orange* his Forces, did great mischiefs to all scatter'd parties of the Duke of *Alva's* Troops in their march through those parts. But after that attempt of the Prince ended without success, and he was forced back into *Germany*; the Count of *Marcke*, a violent and implacable Enemy to the Duke of *Alva* and his Government, with many others of the broken Troops, (whom the same fortune and disposition had left together in *Friezland*,) mann'd out some Ships of small force, and betook themselves to Sea; and, with Commissions from the Prince of *Orange*, began to prey upon all they could master, that belonged to the *Spaniards*. They sometimes sheltered and watered, and sold their Prizes in some Creeks or small Harbors of *England*, though forbidden by Queen *Elizabeth*, (then in Peace with *Spain*) sometimes in the River *Ems*, or some small Ports of *Friezland*; till at length, having gain'd considerable Riches

by these Adventures, whether to sell, or to refresh, whether
driven by storm, or led by design, (upon knowledge of the
ill Blood which the new Taxes had bred in all the Provinces)
they landed in the Island of the *Briel*, assaulted and carried
the Town, pull'd down the Images in the Churches, professed openly their Religion, declared against the Taxes and
Tyranny of the *Spanish* Government, and were immediately
followed by the Revolt of most of the Towns of *Holland*,
Zealand, and *West-Friezland*, who threw out the *Spanish*
Garrisons, renounced their obedience to King *Philip*, and
swore Fidelity to the Prince of *Orange*.

The Prince returned out of *Germany* with new Forces;
and, making use of this fury of the People, contented not
himself with *Holland* and *Zealand*, but marcht up into the
very heart of the Provinces, within five Leagues of *Brussels*,
seizing upon *Mechlin*, and many other Towns, with so
great Consent, Applause, and Concourse of People, that
the whole *Spanish* Dominion seemed now ready to expire
in the *Low-Countries*, if it had not been revived by the
Massacre of the Protestants at *Paris*; which, contrived by
joint Counsels with King *Philip*, and acted by a *Spanish*
party in the Court of *France*, and with so fatal a blow to the
contrary Faction, encouraged the Duke of *Alva*, and dampt
the Prince of *Orange* in the same degree; so that one gathers
strength enough to defend the heart of the Provinces, and
the other retires into *Holland*, and makes that the seat of the
War.

This Country was strong by its nature and seat among the
Waters, that encompass and divide it; but more by a
rougher sort of People at that time, less softned by Trade,
or by Riches; less used to Grants of Money and Taxes;
and proud of their ancient Fame, recorded in the *Roman*

Stories, of being obstinate Defenders of their Liberties, and now most implacable Haters of the *Spanish* Name.

All these dispositions were increased and hardened, in the War that ensued under the Duke of *Alva's* Conduct, or his Sons; by the slaughter of all innocent Persons and Sexes, upon the taking of *Naerden*, where the Houses were burnt, and the Walls levelled to the Ground; by the desperate defence of *Haerlem* for ten Months, with all the practises and returns of ignominy, cruelty, and scorn on both sides; while the very Women listed themselves in Companies, repaired Breaches, gave Alarms, and beat up Quarters, till, all being famisht, four hundred Burgers (after the surrender) were kill'd in cold Blood, among many other examples of an incensed Conqueror; Which made the Humour of the parties grow more desperate, and their hatred to *Spain* and *Alva* incurable.

The same Army broken and forced to rise from before *Alcmaer*, after a long and fierce Siege in *Alva's* time; and from before *Leyden*, in the time of *Requisenes* (where the Boors themselves opened the Sluces, and drown'd the Country, resolving to mischief the *Spaniards*, at the charge of their own ruin,) gave the great turn to Affairs in *Holland*.

The King grows sensible of Danger, and apprehensive of the total defection of the Provinces; *Alva* weary of his Government, finding his violent Councils and Proceedings had raised a Spirit, which was quiet before he came, and was never to be laid any more. The Duke is recalled, and the War goes on under *Requisenes*; who dying suddenly, and without provisions made by the King for a Successor; the Government, by customs of the Country, devolved by way of Interim upon the Great Council, which lasted some time, by the delay of *Don John* of *Austria's* coming, who was declared the new Governour.

But in this Interim, the strength of the Disease appears; for, upon the mutiny of some *Spanish* Troops, for want of their Pay, and their seizing *Alost*, a Town near *Brussels*, the People grow into a rage, the Tradesmen give over their Shops, and the Country-men their Labour, and all run to Arms; In *Brussels* they force the Senate, pull out those Men they knew to be most addicted to the *Spaniards*, kill such of that Nation as they meet in the streets, and all in general cry out for the expulsion of Foreigners out of the *Low-Countries*, and the Assembling of the States; to which the Council is forced to consent. In the mean time, the chief Persons of the Provinces enter into an agreement with the Prince of *Orange*, to carry on the common Affairs of the Provinces by the same Counsels; so as when the Estates assembled at *Ghent*, without any contest, they agreed upon that Act, which was called *The Pacification of* Ghent, in the Year 1576. whereof, the Chief Articles were, *The expulsion of all foreign Soldiers out of the Provinces; Restoring all the ancient Forms of Government; And referring matters of Religion in each Province to the Provincial Estates; And that for performance hereof, the rest of the Provinces should for ever be confederate with* Holland *and* Zealand. And this made the first Period of the *Low-Country* Troubles, proving to King *Philip* a dear Experience, how little the best Conduct, and boldest Armies, are able to withstand the Torrent of a stubborn and enraged People, which ever bears all down before it, till it comes to be divided into different Chanels by Arts, or by Chance; or, till the Springs, which are the Humours that fed it, come to be spent, or dry up of themselves.

The Foreign Forces, refusing to depart, are declared Rebels; whereupon the *Spanish* Troops force and plunder several Towns, and *Antwerp* among the rest, (by advantage of the Cittadel,) with equal Courage and Avarice; and defend themselves in several Holds from the Forces of the States, till *Don John's* arrival at *Luxemburg*, the only Town of the Provinces, where he thought himself safe, as not involved in the defection of the rest.

The Estates refuse to admit him, without his accepting and confirming the Pacification of *Ghent*; which at length he does, by leave from the King, and enters upon the Government with the dismission of all Foreign Troops, which return into *Italy*. But soon after, *Don John*, whether out of Indignation to see himself but a precarious Governour, without force or dependence; or, desiring new occasions of Fame by a War; or, instructed from *Spain* upon new Counsels, takes the occasion of complementing Queen *Margaret* of *Navar* upon her journy out of *France* to the *Spaw*, and on a sudden seizes upon the Castle of *Namur*. Whereupon the Provinces for the third time throw off their Obedience, call the Prince of *Orange* to *Brussels*, where he is made Protector of *Brabant*, by the States of that Province, and preparations are made on both sides for the War: While *Spain* is busie to form new Armies, and draw them together in *Namur* and *Luxemburg*, the only Provinces obedient to that Crown: And all the rest agree to elect a Governour of their own, and send to *Matthias* the Emperor's Brother, to offer him the Charge.

At this time began to be formed the Male-content Party in the *Low-Countries*; which, though agreeing with the rest in their hatred to the *Spaniards*, and defence of their Liberties and Laws, yet were not inclin'd to shake off their

Allegiance to their Prince, nor change their old and establisht Religion: And these were headed by the Duke of
Areschot, and several Great Men, the more averse from a
general defection, by emulation or envy of the Prince of
Orange his Greatness, who was now grown to have all the
influence and credit in the Counsels of the League.

By the assistance of this Party, after *Don John's* sudden
Death, the Duke of *Parma*, succeeding him, gain'd
Strength and Reputation upon his coming to the Govern-
ment, and an entrance upon that great Scene of Glory and
Victory, which made both his Person so renowned, and the
time of his Government signalized by so many Sieges and
Battels, and the reduction of so great a part of the Body of
the Provinces to the subjection of *Spain*.

Upon the growth of this Party, and for distinction from
them, who, persuing a middle and dangerous Counsel,
were at length to become an accession to one of the
Extreams; The more Northern Provinces, meeting by their
Deputies at *Utrecht*, in the Year 1579, framed that Act
or Alliance, which was ever after called *The Union of
Utrecht*; and was the Original Constitution and Frame of
that Commonwealth, which has since been so well known
in the World, by the Name of *The United Provinces*.

This Union was grounded upon the *Spaniards* breach
of the *Pacification* of *Ghent*, and new invasion of some
Towns in *Gelderland*; and was not pretended to divide these
Provinces from the generality, nor from the said *Pacification*; but to strengthen and persue the Ends of it, by more
vigorous and united Counsels and Arms.

The chief force of this Union consists in these Points,
drawn out of the Instrument it self.

The Seven Provinces unite themselves so, as if they were

but one Province, and so, as never to be divided by Testament, Donation, Exchange, Sale, or Agreement: Reserving to each particular Province and City, all Priviledges, Rights, Customs and Statutes; In adjudging whereof, or differences that shall arise between any of the Provinces, the rest shall not intermeddle further, than to intercede towards an Agreement.

They bind themselves to assist one another with Life and Fortunes against all Force and Assault made upon any of them, whether upon pretence of Royal Majesty, of restoring Catholique Religion, or any other whatsoever.

All Frontier-Towns belonging to the Union, if Old, to be fortified at the charge of the Province where they lye; if New, to be erected at the charge of the Generality.

All Imposts and Customs from three Months to three Months, to be offered to them that bid most; and, with the Incomes of the Royal Majesty, to be employed for the common defence.

All Inhabitants to be Listed and Trained within a Month, from 18 to 60 years old. Peace and War not to be made without consent of all the Provinces; Other cases, that concern the management of both, by most Voices. Differences that shall arise upon the first, between the Provinces, to be submitted to the Stadtholders.

Neighbouring-Princes, Lords, Lands, and Cities, to be admitted into the Union, by consent of the Provinces.

For Religion, those of *Holland* and *Zealand* to act in it as seems good unto themselves. The other Provinces may regulate themselves according to the tenor establisht by *Matthias*, or else as they shall judge to be most for the peace and welfare of their particular Provinces; provided, every one remain free in his Religion, and no Man be examined or entrapped for that cause, according to the Pacification of *Ghent*.

In case of any dissention or differences between Provinces, if it concern one in particular, it shall be accommodated by the others; if it concern all in general, by the Stadtholders: In both which cases, Sentence to be pronounced within a Month, and without Appeal or Revision.

The States to be held, as has been formerly used; and the Mint in such manner, as shall hereafter be agreed by all the Provinces.

Interpretation of these Articles to remain in the States; but in case of their differing, in the Stadtholders.

They bind themselves to fall upon, and imprison, any, that shall act contrary to these Articles; in which case no Priviledge nor Exemption to be valid.

This Act was Signed by the Deputies of *Gelderland, Zutphen, Holland, Zealand, Utrecht*, and the Omlands of *Frize, Jan.* 23, 1579. but was not Signed by the Prince of *Orange* till *May* following; and with this Signification, judging, that by the same the Superiority and Authority of Arch-Duke *Matthias* is not lessened.

In the same Year, this Union was enter'd and signed by the Cities of *Ghent, Nimmeguen, Arnhem, Leewarden*, with some particular Nobles of *Friezland, Venlo, Ypres, Antwerp, Breda*, and *Bruges*. And thus these Provinces became a Commonwealth, but in so low and uncertain a state of Affairs, by reason of the various Motions and Affections of Mens Minds, the different Ends and Interests of the several Parties, especially in the other Provinces; and the mighty Power and Preparations of the *Spanish* Monarchy to oppress them, that in their first Coin they caused a Ship to be stamped, labouring among the Waves without Sails or Oars; and these words: *Incertum, quò fata ferant.*

I thought so particular a deduction necessary to discover the natural causes of this Revolution in the *Low-Countries*, which has since had so great a part, for near an hundred years, in all the Actions and Negotiations of Christendom; and to find out the true Incentives of that obstinate love for their Liberties, and invincible hatred for the *Spanish* Nation and Government, which laid the foundation of this Commonwealth: And this last I take to have been the stronger passion, and of the greater effect, both in the bold Counsels of contracting their Union, and the desperate Resolutions of defending it. For not long after, the whole Council of this new State, being prest by the extremities of their Affairs, passing by the form of Government in the way of a Commonwealth, made an earnest and solemn Offer of the Dominion of these Provinces both to *England* and *France*; but were refused by both Crowns: And though they retain'd the Name of a Free People, yet they soon lost the ease of the Liberties they contended for, by the absoluteness of their Magistrates in the several Cities and Provinces, and by the extream pressure of their Taxes, which so long a War, with so mighty an Enemy, made necessary for the support of their State.

But the hatred of the *Spanish* Government, under *Alva*, was so universal, that it made the Revolt general through the Provinces, running through all Religions, and all Orders of Men, as appeared by the Pacification of *Ghent*; Till by the division of the Parties, by the Powers of so vast a Monarchy as *Spain* at that time, and by the matchless Conduct and Valour of the Duke of *Parma*, this Humor, like Poison in a strong Constitution, and with the help of violent Physick, was expell'd from the Heart, which was *Flanders* and *Brabant*, (with the rest of the Ten Provinces) into the outward Members; and by their being cut off, the Body was saved. After which, the most enflamed Spirits being driven by the Arms of *Spain*, or drawn by the hopes of Liberty and Safety, into the *United Provinces* out of the rest, the hatred of *Spain* grew to that heigth, that they were not only willing to submit to any new Dominion, rather than return to the old; but when they could find no Master to protect them, and their Affairs grew desperate, they were once certainly upon the Counsel of burning their great Towns, wasting and drowning what they could of their own Country, and going to seek some new Seats in the *Indies*. Which they might have executed, if they had found Shipping enough to carry off all their Numbers, and had not been detained by the compassion of those which must have been left behind, at the mercy of an incensed and conquering Master.

The *Spanish* and *Italian* Writers content themselves to attribute the causes of these Revolutions to the change of Religion, to the native stubbornness of the People, and to the Ambition of the Princes of *Orange*: But Religion, without mixtures of Ambition and Interest, works no such violent effects; and produces rather the Examples of constant sufferings, than of desperate Actions. The nature of the People cannot change of a sudden, no more than the Climate which infuses it; and no Country hath brought forth better Subjects, than many of these Provinces, both before and since these Commotions among them: And the Ambition of one Man could neither have designed or atchieved so great an Adventure, had it not been seconded with universal Discontent: Nor could that have been raised to so great an heighth and heat, without so many circumstances as fell in from an unhappy course of the *Spanish* Counsels, to kindle and foment it. For though it had been hard to Head such a Body, and give it so strong a Principle of Life, and so regular Motions, without the accident of so great a Governour in the Provinces, as Prince *William* of *Orange*; A Man of equal Abilities in Council and in Arms; Cautious and Resolute, Affable and Severe, Supple to occasions, and yet Constant to his Ends; of mighty Revenues and Dependence in the Provinces, of great Credit and Alliance in *Germany*; esteemed and honoured abroad, but at home infinitely lov'd and trusted by the People, who thought him affectionate to their Country, sincere in his Professions and Designs, able and willing to defend their Liberties, and unlikely to invade them by any Ambition of his own. Yet all these Qualities might very well have been confin'd to the Duty and Services of a Subject, as they were in *Charles* the Fifth's time; Without the absence of the King, and the Peoples Opinion of his Ill-will to their Nation and their Laws; Without the continuance of Foreign Troops after the Wars were ended; The erecting of the new Bishops Sees, and introducing the *Inquisition*; The sole Ministry of *Granvel*, and exclusion of the Lords from their usual part in Councils and Affairs; The Government of a Man so hated, as the Duke of *Alva*; The rigor of his Prosecutions, and the insolence of his Statue: And lastly, Without the death of *Egmont*, and the imposition of the Tenth and Twentieth part, against the Legal forms of Government in a Country, where a long derived Succession had made the People fond and tenacious of their ancient Customs and Laws.

These were the seeds of their hatred to *Spain*; which, increasing by the course of about Threescore years War, was not allay'd by a long succeeding Peace; but will appear to have been an Ingredient into the Fall, as it was into the Rise, of this State; which, having been thus planted, came to be conserved and cultivated by many Accidents and Influences from abroad: But those having had no part in the Constitution of their State, nor the Frame of their Government; I will content my self to mention only the chief of them, which most contributed to preserve the Infancy of this Commonwealth, and make way for its growth. The Causes of its succeeding Greatness and Riches being not to be sought for in the Events of their Wars, but in the Institutions and Orders of their Government, their Customs and Trade, which will make the Arguments of the ensuing Chapters.

When *Don John* threw off the Conditions he had at first accepted of the Pacification of *Ghent*, and by the surprize of *Namur* broke into Arms; The Estate of the Provinces offer'd the Government of their Country to *Matthias*, Brother to the Emperor, as a temper between their return to the Obedience of *Spain*, and the Popular Government which was moulding in the Northern Provinces. But *Matthias* arriving without the advice or support of the Emperor, or Credit in the Provinces; and having the Prince of *Orange* given him for his Lieutenant-General, was only a Cypher, and his Government a piece of Pageantry, which past without effect, and was soon ended; So that, upon the Duke of *Parma's* taking on him the Government, some new Protection was necessary to this Infant-State, that had not Legs to support it against such a storm, as was threatned upon the return of the *Spanish* and *Italian* Forces, to make the Body of a formidable Army, which the Duke of *Parma* was forming in *Namur* and *Luxemburgh*.

Since the Conference of *Bayonne* between the Queen-Mother of *France*, and her Daughter Queen of *Spain*; Those two Crowns had continued, in the Reign of *Francis* and *Charles*, to assist one another in the common Design there agreed on, of prosecuting with violence those they called the Hereticks, in both their Dominions. The Peace held constant, if not kind, between *England* and *Spain*; so as King *Philip* had no Wars upon his hands in Christendom, during these Commotions in the *Low-Countries*; And the boldness of their Confederates, in their first Revolt and Union, seemed greater at such a time, than the success of their Resistances afterwards, when so many occasions fell in to weaken and divert the Forces of the *Spanish* Monarchy.

For *Henry* the Third coming to the Crown of *France*, and at first only fetter'd and controul'd by the Faction of the *Guises*, but afterwards engaged in an open War, (which They had raised against him, upon pretext of preserving the Catholique Religion, and in a conjunction of Counsels with *Spain*) was forced into better measures with the *Hugonots* of his Kingdom, and fell into ill intelligence with *Philip* the Second, so as Queen *Elizabeth* having declined to undertake openly the protection of the *Low-Country* Provinces, It was, by the concuring resolution of the States, and the consent of the *French* Court, devolved upon the Duke of *Alencon*, Brother to *Henry* the Third.

But this Prince entred *Antwerp* with an ill presage to the *Flemings*, by an attempt which a *Biscainer* made, the same day, upon the Prince of *Orange's* Life, shooting him, though not mortally, in the Head: And He continued his short Government with such mutual distasts between the *French* and the *Flemings*, (the Heat and Violence of one Nation agreeing ill with the Customs and Liberties of the other,) that the Duke, attempting to make himself absolute Master of the City of *Antwerp* by force, was driven out of the Town, and thereupon retired out of the Country, with extream resentment of the *Flemings*, and indignation of the *French*; so as the Prince of *Orange* being not long after Assasin'd at *Delph*, and the Duke of *Parma* encreasing daily in Reputation and in Force, and the Male-content Party falling back apace to his Obedience, an end was presaged by most Men to the Affairs of the Confederates.

But the Root was deeper, and not so easily shaken: For the *United Provinces*, after the unhappy Transactions with the *French*, under the Duke of *Alencon*, reassumed their Union in 1583. binding themselves, in case, by fury of the War, any point of it had not been observed, to endeavour from that time to see it effected: In case any doubt had happened, to see it clear'd: And any Difficulties, composed: And in regard, the Article concerning Religion had been so fram'd in the Union, because in all the other Provinces, besides *Holland* and *Zealand*, the *Romish* Religion was then used, but now the *Evangelical*; It was agreed by all the Provinces of the Union, That, from this time in them all, the Evangelical Reformed Religion should alone be openly Preached and Exercised.

They were so far from being broken in their Designs by the Prince of *Orange's* death, That they did all the Honour that could be to his Memory, substituted Prince *Maurice* his Son, though but Sixteen years old, in all his Honours and Commands, and obstinately refused all overtures that were made them of Peace; resolving upon all the most desperate Actions and Sufferings, rather than return under the *Spanish* Obedience.

But these Spirits were fed and heighten'd, in a great

degree, by the hopes and countenance given them about this time from *England*: For Queen *Elizabeth*, and *Philip* the Second, though they still preserved the Name of Peace, yet had worn out, in a manner, the Effects as well as the Dispositions of it, whilst the *Spaniard* fomented and assisted the Insurrections of the *Irish*, and Queen *Elizabeth* the new Commonwealth in the *Low-Countries*; though neither directly, yet by Countenance, Money, voluntary Troops, and ways that were equally felt on both sides, and equally understood.

King *Philip* had lately increased the greatness of his Empire, by the Inheritance or Invasion of the Kingdoms of *Portugal*, upon King *Sebastian's* loss in *Africa*; But I know not whether he had encreas'd his Power, by the accession of a Kingdom, with disputed Title, and a discontented People, who could neither be used like good Subjects and governed without Armies; nor like a Conquered Nation, and so made to bear the charge of their forced Obedience; But this addition of Empire, with the vast Treasure flowing every year out of the *Indies*, had without question raised King *Philip's* Ambition to vaster designs; which made him embrace at once, the protection of the League in *France* against *Henry* the Third and Fourth; and the Donation made him of *Ireland* by the Pope; and so embarque himself in a War with both those Crowns, while He was bearded with the open Arms and defiance of his own Subjects in the *Low-Countries*.

But 'tis hard to be imagin'd, how far the Spirit of one Great Man goes in the Fortunes of any Army or State. The Duke of *Parma* coming to the Government without any footing in more than two of the smallest Provinces, collecting an Army from *Spain*, *Italy*, *Germany*, and the broken

Troops of the Country left him by *Don John*, having all the other Provinces confederated against him, and both *England* and *France* beginning to take open part in their defence; yet, by force of his own Valour, Conduct, and the Discipline of his Army, with the dis-interested and generous Qualities of his Mind, winning equally upon the Hearts and Arms of the Revolted Countries, and piercing through the Provinces with an uninterrupted course of Successes, and the recovery of the most important Towns in *Flanders*; At last, by the taking of *Antwerp* and *Groningue*, reduced the Affairs of the Union to so extreme distress, that, being grown destitute of all hopes and succors from *France*, (then deep engaged in their own Civil Wars,) They threw themselves wholly at the Feet of Queen *Elizabeth*, imploring her Protection, and offering her the Sovereignty of their Country. The Queen refused the Dominion, but enter'd into Articles with their Deputies in 1585. obliging her Self to very great Supplies of Men and of Moneys, lent them upon the security of the *Briel, Flushing*, and *Ramekins*; which were performed, and Sir *John Norrice* sent over to command her Forces; and afterwards in 87, upon the War broken out with *Spain*, and the mighty threats of the *Spanish* Armada, she sent over yet greater Forces under the Earl of *Leicester*, whom the States admitted, and swore Obedience to him, as Governour of their *United Provinces*.

But this Government lasted not long, distasts and suspicions soon breaking out between *Leicester* and the States; partly from the jealousie of his affecting an Absolute Dominion, and Arbitrary disposal of all Offices; But chiefly, of the Queens intentions to make a Peace with *Spain*; and the easie loss of some of their Towns, by Governors placed in them by the Earl of *Leicester*,

encreased their Discontents. Notwithstanding this ill intercourse, the Queen re-assures them in both those Points,
disapproves some of *Leicester's* proceedings, receives franc
and hearty assistances from them in her Naval Preparations,
against the *Spaniards*; and at length, upon the disorders
encreasing between the Earl of *Leicester* and the States,
commands him to resign his Government, and release the
States of the Oath they had taken to obey him. And after
all this had past, the Queen easily sacrificing all particular
resentments to the interest of her Crown, continued her
Favour, Protection and Assistances, to the States, during the
whole course of Her Reign, which were return'd with the
greatest deference and veneration to her Person, that was
ever paid by them to any Foreign Prince, and continues still
to Her Name in the remembrance, and frequently in the
mouths, of all sorts of People among them.

After *Leicester's* departure, Prince *Maurice* was, by the
consent of the Union, chosen their Governour, but with a
reservation to Queen *Elizabeth*; and enter'd that Command
with the hopes, which he made good in the execution of it
for many years; proving the greatest Captain of his Age,
famous, particularly, in the Discipline and Ordonance of
his Armies, and the ways of Fortification by him first
invented or perfected, and since his time imitated by all.

But the great breath that was given the States in the heat
of their Affairs, was by the sharp Wars made by Queen
Elizabeth upon the *Spaniards* at Sea in the *Indies*, and the
Expedition of *Lisbon* and *Cadiz*, and by the declining
Affairs of the League in *France*, for whose support *Philip*
the Second was so passionately engaged, that twice he
commanded the Duke of *Parma* to interrupt the course of
his Victories in the *Low-Countries*, and march into *France*

for the relief of *Roan* and *Paris*; which much augmented the
Renown of this great Captain, but as much impaired the
state of the *Spanish* Affairs in *Flanders*. For in the Duke of
Parma's absence, Prince *Maurice* took in all the places held
by the *Spaniard* on t'other side the *Rhine*, which gave them
entrance into the *United Provinces*.

The succession of *Henry* the Fourth to the Crown of
France, gave a mighty blow to the Designs of King *Philip*;
and a much greater, The general obedience and acknowledgment of him upon his change of Religion. With this King,
the States began to enter a confidence and kindness, and the
more by that which interceded between Him and the Queen
of *England*, who had all their dependance during her life;
But, after her death, King *Henry* grew to have greater
credit than ever in the *United Provinces*; though, upon the
decay of the *Spanish* Power under the Ascendent of this
King, the States fell into very early jealousies of his growing
too great and too near them in *Flanders*.

With the Duke of *Parma* died all the Discipline, and,
with that, all the Fortunes, of the *Spanish* Arms in *Flanders*;
The frequent Mutinies of their Soldiers, dangerous in
effect and in example, were more talkt of, than any other
of their actions, in the short Government of *Mansfield*,
Ernest, and *Fuentes*. Till the old Discipline of their Armies
began to revive, and their Fortune a little to respire under
the new Government of Cardinal *Albert*, who came into
Flanders both Governour and Prince of the *Low-Countries*,
in the head of a mighty Army drawn out of *Germany* and
Italy, to try the last effort of the *Spanish* Power, either in
a prosperous War, or, at least, in making way for a necessary
Peace.

But the choice of the Arch-Duke, and this new Authority,

had a deeper root, and design, than at first appear'd: For that mighty King *Philip* the Second, born to so vast Possessions, and to so much vaster Desires, after a long dream of raising his Head into the Clouds, found it now ready to lye down in the Dust: His Body broken with Age and Infirmities, his Mind with Cares and distemper'd Thoughts, and the Royal servitude of a solicitous life; He began to see, in the glass of Time and Experience, the true shapes of all human Greatness and Designs; And, finding to what airy Figures he had hitherto sacrificed his Health, and Ease, and the Good of his Life, He now turn'd his Thoughts wholly to Rest and Quiet, which he had never yet allowed either the World, or Himself: His Designs upon *England*, and his Invincible Armada, had ended in smoak: Those upon *France*, in Events the most contrary to what he had proposed: And instead of mastering the Liberties, and breaking the Stomach, of his *Low-Country* Subjects, he had lost Seven of his Provinces, and held the rest by the tenure of a War, that cost him more than they were worth. He had made lately a Peace with *England*, and desir'd it with *France*; and though he scorn'd it with his revolted Subjects in his own Name, yet he wish'd it in anothers; and was unwilling to entail a quarrel upon his Son, which had crost his Fortunes, and busied his Thoughts all the course of his Reign. He therefore resolved to commit these two Designs to the management of Arch-Duke *Albert*, with the style of Governor and Prince of the *Low-Countries*; to the end, that, if he could reduce the Provinces to their old subjection, He should Govern them as *Spanish* Dominions; If that was once more in vain attempted, He should by a Marriage with *Clara Isabella Eugenia* (King *Philip's* beloved Daughter) receive these Provinces as a Dowry, and become the

Prince of them, with a condition only, of their returning to *Spain*, in case of *Isabella's* dying without Issue. King *Philip* believed, that the Presence of a natural Prince among his Subjects; That the Birth and Customs of Arch-Duke *Albert*, being a *German*; The generous and obliging dispositions of *Isabella*, might gain further upon this stubborn People, than all the Force and Rigor of his former Counsels: And at the worst; That they might make a Peace, if they could not a War, and without interesting the Honour and Greatness of the *Spanish* Crown.

In persuit of this determination, like a wise King, while he intended nothing but Peace, He made Preparations, as if he design'd nothing but War; knowing, that his own desires of Peace would signifie nothing, unless he could force his Enemies to desire it too. He therefore sent the Arch-Duke into *Flanders*, at the head of such an Army, that, believing the Peace with *France* must be the first in order, and make way for either the War or Peace afterward in the *Low-Countries*, He marcht into *France*, and took *Amiens* the chief City of *Picardy*, and thereby gave such an alarm to the *French* Court, as they little expected; and had never received in the former Wars. But while *Albert* bent the whole force of the War upon *France*, till he determin'd it in a Peace with that Crown, Prince *Maurice*, who had taken *Groningue* in the time of *Ernest*, now mastered *Linghen*, *Groll*, and other places in *Overyssel*, thereby adding those Provinces intire, to the Body of the Union; and at *Albert's* return into *Flanders*, entertain'd him with the Battel of *Newport*, won by the desperate Courage of the *English*, under Sir *Francis Vere*, where *Albert* was wounded, and very near being taken.

After this Loss, the Arch-Duke was yet comforted and

relieved by the obsequious Affections and Obedience of his new Subjects, so far as to resolve upon the Siege of *Ostend*; which having some time continued, and being almost disheartned by the strength of the place, and invincible Courage of the Defendants, He was recruited by a Body of Eight thousand *Italians*, under the Marquess *Spinola*, to whom the prosecution of this Siege was committed: He took the place, after Three years Siege, not by any want of Men or Provisions within, (the Haven, and relief by Sea, being open all the time;) but perfectly for want of ground, which was gain'd foot by foot, till not so much was left, as would hold Men to defend it; a great example, how impossible it is to defend any Town, that cannot be relieved by an Army strong enough to raise the Siege.

Prince *Maurice*, though he could not save *Ostend*, made yet amends for its loss, by the taking of *Grave* and *Sluyce*; so as the *Spaniards* gain'd little but the honour of the Enterprize: And *Philip* the Second being dead, about the time of the Arch-Dukes and Dutchesses arrival in *Flanders*, and, with him the personal resentment of that War, the Arch-Duke, by consent of the *Spanish* Court, began to apply his Thoughts wholly to a Peace; which another circumstance had made more necessary, than any of those already mentioned.

As the *Dutch* Commonwealth was born out of the Sea, so out of the same Element it drew its first strength and consideration, as well as afterwards its Riches and Greatness: For before the Revolts, the Subjects of the *Low-Countries*, though never allowed the Trade of the *Indies*, but in the *Spanish* Fleets, and under *Spanish* Covert, yet many of them had in that manner made the Voyages, and become skilful Pilots, as well as vers'd in the ways, and sensible of the infinite gains of that Trade. And after the Union, a greater confluence of People falling down into the *United Provinces*, than could manage their Stock, or find employment at Land; Great multitudes turn'd their endeavours to Sea; and, having lost the Trade of *Spain* and the *Streights*, fell not only into That of *England, France*, and the Northern Seas, but ventur'd upon That of the *East-Indies*, at first with small Forces and Success; But in course of time, and by the Institution of an *East-India* Company, This came to be persued with so general application of the Provinces, and so great advantage, that they made themselves Masters of most of the Colonies and Forts planted there by the *Porteguesses* (now Subjects of *Spain.*) The *Dutch* Seamen grew as well acquainted with those vast Seas and Coasts, as with their own; and *Holland* became the great Magazine of all the Commodities of those Eastern Regions.

In the *West-Indies* their attempts were neither so frequent nor prosperous, the *Spanish* Plantations there being too numerous and strong; But by the multitude of their Shipping, set out with publique or private Commissions, they infested the Seas, and began to wait for, and threaten, the *Spanish Indian* Fleets, and sometimes to attempt their Coasts in that new World (which was to touch *Spain* in the most sensible part,) and gave their Court the strongest motives to endeavor a Peace, that might secure those Treasures in their way, and preserve them in *Spain*, by stopping the issue of those vast Sums, which were continually transmitted to entertain the *Low-Country* Wars.

These Respects gave the first rise to a Treaty of Peace, the Proposal whereof came wholly from the *Spaniards*; and the very mention of it could hardly at first be fast'ned upon the States; nor could they ever be prevail'd with to make way for any Negotiation by a suspension of Arms, till the Arch-Duke had declared, He would treat with them as with free Provinces, upon whom, neither He, nor *Spain* had any pretence. However, the Affair was persued with so much Art and Industry on the Arch-Dukes part, and with so passionate Desires of the *Spanish* Court, to end this War, That they were content to Treat it at the *Hague*, the Seat of the States-General; And, for the greater Honour, and better Conduct of the whole Business, appointed the four chief Ministers of the Arch-Dukes, Their Commissioners to attend and persue it there; who were, Their Camp-Master-General *Spinola*, The President of the Council, and the Two Secretaries of State and of War in *Flanders*.

On the other side, in *Holland* all the Paces towards this Treaty were made with great coldness and arrogance, raising punctilious difficulties upon every word of the Arch-Dukes Declaration of Treating them as Free Provinces, and upon *Spain's* Ratification of that Form; And forcing them to send Expresses into *Spain*, upon every occasion, and to attend the length of those Returns. For the prosperous success of their Arms at Land, in the course of above Thirty years War and the mighty growth of their Naval Power, and (under that Protection) of their Trade, had made the whole Body of their Militia, both at Land and Sea, averse from this Treaty, as well as the greatest part of the People; whose inveterate hatred against *Spain* was still as fierce as ever; and who had the hopes or dispositions of raising their Fortunes by the War, whereof they had so many and great Examples among them.

But there was, at the bottom, one Foreign, and another Domestick, Consideration, which made way for this

Treaty, more than all those Arguments that were the common Theams, or than all the Offices of the Neighbour-Princes, who concerned themselves in this Affair, either from Interest of their own, or the Desires of ending a War, which had so long exercised, in a manner, the Arms of all Christendom upon the Stage of the *Low-Countries.* The Greatness of the *Spanish* Monarchy, so formidable under *Charles* the Fifth, and *Philip* the Second, began now to decline by the vast Designs, and unfortunate Events, of so many ambitious Counsels: And, on the other side, the Affairs of *Henry* the Fourth of *France* were now at the greatest Height and Felicity, after having atchieved so many Adventures, with incredible Constancy and Valour, and ended all his Wars in a Peace with *Spain.* The *Dutch* imagin'd, that the hot spirits of the *French* could not continue long without some exercise; and that to prevent it at home, it might be necessary for that King to give it them abroad; That no enterprize lay so convenient for Him, as that upon *Flanders,* which had anciently been part of the *Gallick* Nation, and whose first Princes derived and held of the Kings of *France.* Besides, they had intimations, that *Henry* the Fourth was taken up in great Preparations for War, which they doubted would at one time or other fall on that side, at least, if they were invited by any greater decays of the *Spanish* Power in *Flanders*: And they knew very well, they should lye as much at the mercy of such a Neighbor as *France,* as they had formerly done of such a Master as *Spain.* For the *Spanish* Power in *Flanders* was fed by Treasures that came by long and perillous Voyages out of *Spain*; By Troops drawn either from thence, or from *Italy* or *Germany,* with much casualty, and more expence: Their Territory of the Ten Provinces was small, and awed by the Neighborhood and Jealousies both of *England* and *France*. But if *France* were once Master of *Flanders*, the Body of that Empire would be so great, and so entire; so abounding in People, and in Riches, that whenever they found, or made, an occasion of invading the *United Provinces*, they had no hopes of preserving themselves by any opposition or diversion: And the end of their mighty resistances against *Spain* was, to have no Master; and not to change one for another, as they should do in this case: Therefore the most Intelligent among their Civil Ministers thought it safest, by a Peace, to give breath to the Arch-Duke's and *Spanish* Power, and by that means, to lessen the invitation of the Arms of *France* into *Flanders*, under so great a King.

For what was Domestique, The Credit and Power of Prince *Maurice*, built at first upon that of his Father, but much raised by his own Personal Virtues and Qualities, and the success of his Arms, was now grown so high (the Prince being Governor, or Stadtholder, of Four of the Provinces, and Two of his Cousins of the other Three,) that several of the States, headed by *Barnevelt*, Pensioner of *Holland*, and a Man of great Abilities and Authority among them, became jealous of the Prince's Power, and pretended to fear the growth of it to an absolute Dominion: They knew, it would increase by the continuance of a War, which was wholly managed by the Prince; and thought, that in a Peace it would diminish, and give way to the Authority of Civil Power: Which disposed this whole Party to desire the Treaty, and to advance the progress and issue of it by all their assistances. And these different humors stirring in the Heart of the States, with almost equal strength and vigor; The Negotiation of a Peace came to be eluded, after long debates and infinite endeavours; Breaking, in appearance, upon the points of Religion, and the *Indian* Trade: But yet came to knit again, and conclude in a Truce of Twelve years, dated in the year 1609. whereof the most essential points were, The Declaration of Treating with them as Free Provinces; The Cessation of all Acts of Hostility on both sides, during the Truce; The enjoyment for that space, of all that each party possest at the time of the Treaty; That no new Fortification should be raised on either side: And that free Commerce should be restored on all parts in the same manner, as it was before the Wars.

And thus the State of the *United Provinces* came to be acknowledged, as a Free Common-wealth by their ancient Master, having before been Treated so by most of the Kings and Princes of *Europe*, in frequent Ambassies and Negotiations. Among which, a particular preference was given to the *English* Crown, whose Ambassador had Session and Vote in their Council of State, by Agreement with Queen *Elizabeth*, and in acknowledgment of those great Assistances, which gave life to their State, when it was upon the point of expiring: Though the *Dutch* pretend, that Priviledge was given to the Ambassador, by virtue of the Possession this Crown had of the *Briel, Flussigue*, and *Ramekins*; and that it was to cease upon the restitution of those Towns, and repayment of those Sums lent by the Queen.

In the very time of Treating this Truce, a League was concluded between *Henry* the Fourth of *France*, and the States, for preserving the Peace, if it came to be concluded; or, in case of its failing, for assistance of one another, with Ten thousand Men on the Kings part, and Five thousand on the States. Nor did that King make any difficulty of continuing the two Regiments of Foot, and Two hundred Horse in the States Service, at his own charge, after the Truce, which he had maintained for several years before it; Omitting no provisions that might tye that State to his Interests, and make him at present Arbiter of the Peace, and for the future of the War, if the Truce should come to be broken, or to expire of itself.

By what has been related, it will easily appear, That no State was ever born with stronger Throws, or nurst up with harder fare, or inur'd to greater Labours or Dangers in the whole course of its Youth; which are circumstances that usually make strong and healthy Bodies: And so this has proved, having never had more than one Disease break out, in the space of Ninety three years, which may be accounted the Age of this State, reckoning from the Union of *Utrecht*, enter'd by the Provinces in 1579. But this Disease, like those of the Seed, or Conception, in a natural Body, Though it first appear'd in *Barnevelt's* time, breaking out upon the Negotiations with *Spain*, and seemed to end with his death, (who was beheaded not many years after;) yet has it ever since continued lurking in the Veins of this State, and appearing upon all Revolutions, that seem to favour the predominancy of the one or other Humor in the Body; And under the Names of the Prince of *Orange's*, and the *Arminian*, Party, has ever made the weak side of this State; and whenever their Period comes, will prove the occasion of their Fall.

The ground of this name of *Arminian* was, That whilst *Barnevelt's* Party accused those of the Prince of *Orange's*, as being careless of their Liberties, so dearly bought; as devoted to the House of *Orange*; and disposed to the admission of an absolute Principality, and in order thereunto, as promoters of a perpetual War with *Spain*: So those of the Prince's Party, accused the others, as leaning still to, and looking kindly upon, their old servitude, and relishing the *Spaniard*, both in their Politicks, by so eagerly affecting a Peace with that Crown; and in their Religion, by being generally *Arminians*, (which was esteemed the middle part between the *Calvinists* and the *Roman* Religion.) And besides these mutual Reproaches, the two Parties have ever valued themselves upon the asserting, one of the true and purer Reformed Religion; and the other, of the truer and freer Liberties of the State.

The Fortunes of this Commonwealth, that have happened in their Wars or Negotiations, since the Truce with *Spain*, and what Circumstances or Accidents, both abroad and at home, serv'd to cultivate their mighty growth, and conspired to the Greatness wherein they appear'd to the World in the beginning of the year 1665. being not only the subject of the Relations, but even the Observations, of this present Age; I shall either leave, as more obvious, and less necessary to the account I intend of the Civil Government of this Common-wealth: Or else reserve them till the same vein of Leisure or Humour invite me to continue this Deduction to this present time; The Affairs of this State having been complicated with all the variety and memorable Revolutions, both of Actions and Counsels, that have since happened in the rest of Christendom.

In the mean time, I will close this Relation with an Event, which arrived soon after the conclusion of the Truce, and had like to have broken it within the very year, if not prevented by the Offices of the Neighbour Princes, but more by a change of Humour in the United States, conspiring to the conservation of the new-restored Peace in these parts of the World.

In the end of the year 1609. dyed the Duke of *Cleves* and *Juliers*, without Heir-male, leaving those Dutchies to the pretensions of his Daughters, in whose Right the Duke of *Brandenburgh* and *Nieuburgh* possessed themselves of such parts of those Territories, as they first could invade; each of them pretending right to the whole Inheritance. *Brandenburgh* seeks Protection and Favour to his Title, from the *United Provinces*; *Nieuburg* from Arch-Duke *Albert*, and from *Spain*. The Arch-Duke, newly respiring from so long a War, had no desire to interess himself in this Quarrel, further than the care, that the *Dutch* should not take advantage of it; and, under pretext of assisting one of the parties, seize upon some of those Dominions lying contiguous to their own. The *Dutch* were not so equal, nor content to lose so fair an occasion, and surprized the Town of *Juliers* (though pretending only to keep it till the parties agreed.) And believing that *Spain*, after having parted with so much in the late Truce, to end a quarrel of their own, would not venture a breach of it upon a quarrel of their Neighbours. But the Arch-Duke, having first taken his measures with *Spain*, and foreseeing the consequence of this Affair, resolved to venture the whole State of *Flanders* in a new War, rather than suffer such an encrease of Power and Dominion to the States. And thereupon, First, in the behalf of the Duke of *Nieuburgh*, requires from them the restitution of *Juliers*; and upon their artificious and dilatory Answers, immediately draws his Forces together, and with an Army, under the Command of *Spinola*, marches towards *Juliers*, (which the States were in no care of, as well provided for a bold defence;) But makes a sudden turn, and sits down before *Wesel*, with such a terror and surprize to the Inhabitants, that he carries the Town before the *Dutch* could come in to their assistance. *Wesel* was a strong Town upon the *Rhine*, which the Duke of *Brandenburgh* pretended to, as belonging to the Dutchy of *Cleve*; but the Citizens held it at this time as an Imperial Town, and under protection of the *Dutch*; Who, amazed at this sudden and bold attempt of *Spinola*, which made him Master of a Pass that lay fair for any further Invasion upon their Provinces, (especially those on t'other side the *Rhine*,) engage the Offices of both the *English* and *French* Crowns, to mediate an Agreement, which at length they conclude, so as neither party should, upon any pretence, draw their Forces into any part of these Dutchies. Thus the Arch-Duke having by the fondness of Peace, newly made a Truce, upon Conditions imposed by the *Dutch*; now by the Resolution of making War, obtains a Peace, upon the very Terms proposed by himself, and by *Spain*. An Event of great Instruction and Example, how dangerous it ever proves for weak Princes to call in greater to their aid, which makes them a Prey to their Friend, instead of their Enemy; How the only time of making an advantageous Peace, is, when your Enemy desires it, and when you are in the best condition of pursuing a War: And how vain a Counsel it is, to avoid a War, by yielding any point of Interest or Honour; which does but invite new Injuries, encourage Enemies, and dishearten Friends.

CHAPTER II

Of their Government

It is evident by what has been discoursed in the former Chapter concerning the Rise of this State, (which is to be dated from the Union of *Utrecht*,) that it cannot properly be styled a Commonwealth, but is rather a Confederacy of Seven Sovereign Provinces united together for their common and mutual defence, without any dependance one upon the other. But to discover the nature of their Government from the first springs and motions, It must be taken yet into smaller pieces, by which it will appear, that each of these Provinces is likewise composed of many little States or Cities, which have several marks of Sovereign Power within themselves, and are not subject to the Sovereignty of their Province; Not being concluded in many things by the majority, but only by the universal concurrence of Voices in the Provincial States. For as the States-General cannot make War or Peace, or any new Alliance, or Levies of Money, without the consent of every Province; so cannot the States-Provincial conclude of any of those points, without the consent of each of the Cities, that, by their Constitution, has a Voice in that Assembly. And though in many Civil Causes there lies an Appeal from the Common Judicature of the Cities, to the Provincial Courts of Justice; yet in Criminal, there lies none at all; nor can the Soveraignty of a Province exercise any Judicature, seize upon any Offender, or pardon any Offence within the Jurisdiction of a City, or execute any common Resolution or Law, but by the Justice and Officers of the City itself. By this, a

certain Soveraignty in each City is discerned, the chief
marks whereof are, The Power of exercising Judicature,
levying of Money, and making War and Peace: For the
other, of Coining Money, is neither in particular Cities or
Provinces, but in the generality of the Union, by common
Agreement.

The main Ingredients therefore into the Composition of
this State, are the Freedom of the Cities, the Soveraignty
of the Provinces, the Agreements or Constitutions of the
Union, and the Authority of the Princes of *Orange*; Which
make the Order I shall follow in the Account intended of
this Government. But whereas, the several Provinces in the
Union, and the several Cities in each Province, as they have,
in their Orders and Constitutions, some particular differences, as well as a general resemblance; and the account of
each distinctly would swell this Discourse out of measure,
and to little purpose; I shall confine my self to the account
of *Holland*, as the richest, strongest, and of most Authority
among the Provinces; and of *Amsterdam*, as that which has
the same Preheminencies among the Cities.

The Soveraign Authority of the City of *Amsterdam*[1],
consists, in the Decrees or Results of their Senate, which is
composed of Six and thirty Men, by whom the Justice is
administred, according to ancient forms; in the names of
Officers, and Places of Judicature. But Monies are Levied
by Arbitrary Resolutions, and Proportions, according to
what appears convenient or necessary upon the change or
emergency of occasions. These Senators are for their lives,
and the Senate was anciently chosen by the Voices of the
richer Burghers, or Freemen of the City, who upon the
death of a Senator met together, either in a Church, a

---

[1] Government of the City of *Amsterdam*.

Market, or some other place spacious enough to receive their numbers; and there made an election of the person to succeed, by the majority of Voices. But about a hundred and thirty, or forty years ago, when the Towns of *Holland* began to increase in circuit, and in People, so as those frequent Assemblies grew into danger of tumult and disorders upon every occasion, by reason of their Numbers and Contention; This election of Senators came, by the resolution of the Burghers, in one of their General Assemblies, to be devolved for ever, upon the standing-Senate at that time; So, as ever since, when any one of their number dyes, a new one is chosen by the rest of the Senate, without any intervention of the other Burghers; Which makes the Government a sort of *Oligarchy*, and very different from a popular Government, as it is generally esteemed by those, who, passing or living in these Countries, content themselves with common Observations, or Inquiries. And this resolution of the Burghers, either was agreed upon, or followed by general Consent or Example, about the same time, in all the Towns of the Province, though with some difference in number of their Senators.

By this Senate are chosen the chief Magistrates of the Town, which are the Burgomasters, and the Eschevins: The Burgomasters of *Amsterdam* are Four, whereof three are chosen every year; so as one of them stays in Office two Years; but the three last chosen, are called the *Reigning-Burgomasters* for that Year, and preside by turns, after the first three Months; for so long after a new Election, the Burgomaster of the year before presides; in which time it is supposed the new ones will grow instructed in the Forms and Duties of their Office, and acquainted with the state of the Cities Affairs.

The Burgomasters are chosen by most voices of all those Persons in the Senate, who have been either Burgomasters or Eschevins; and their Authority resembles that of the Lord Mayor and Aldermen in our Cities. They represent the Dignity of the Government, and do the Honour of the City upon all occasions: They dispose of all Under-Offices that fall in their time; and issue out all Monies out of the common Stock or Treasure, judging alone what is necessary for the Safety, Convenience, or Dignity of the City. They keep the Key of the Bank of *Amsterdam*, (the common Treasure of so many Nations,) which is never open'd without the Presence of one of them; And they inspect and persue all the great Publick Works of the City, as the *Ramparts* and *Stadt-house*, now almost finished, with so great Magnificence, and so vast Expence.

This Office is a Charge of the greatest Trust, Authority, and Dignity; and so much the greater, by not being of Profit or Advantage, but only as a way to other constant employments in the City, that are so. The Salary of a Burgomaster of *Amsterdam*, is but Five hundred Gilders a year, though there are Offices worth Five thousand in their disposal; But yet none of them known to have taken Money upon such occasions, which would lose all their Credit in the Town, and thereby their Fortunes by any Publick Employments. They are obliged to no sort of ex-pence, more than ordinary modest Citizens, in their Habits, their Attendance, their Tables, or any part of their own Domestick. They are upon all Publick Occasions waited on by Men in Salary from the Town; and whatever Feasts they make upon Solemn days, or for the Entertainment of any Princes or Foreign Ministers, the Charge is defrayed out of the Common Treasure; but proportioned by their own discretion. At other times, they appear in all places with the simplicity and modesty of other private Citizens. When the Burgomaster's Office expires, they are of course disposed into the other Charges or Employments of the Town, which are very many and beneficial; unless they lose their Credit with the Senate, by any want of Diligence or Fidelity in the discharge of their Office, which seldom arrives.

The *Eschevins* are the Court of Justice in every Town. They are at *Amsterdam* nine in Number; of which Seven are chosen Annually; but two of the preceding year continue in Office. A double number is named by the Senate, out of which the Burgomasters now chuse, as the Prince of *Orange* did in the former Constitution. They are Soveraign Judges in all Criminal Causes. In Civil, after a certain value, there lies Appeal to the Court of Justice of the Province. But they pass sentence of Death upon no Man, without first advising with the Burgomasters; though, after that form is past, they proceed themselves, and are not bound to follow the Burgomasters opinion, but are left to their own: This being only a care or favour of Supererogation to the Life of Man, which is so soon cut off, and never to be retrieved or made amends for.

Under these Soveraign Magistrates, the chief subordinate Officers of the Town, are the Treasurers, who receive and issue out all Moneys that are properly the Revenues or Stock of the City: The *Scout*, who takes care of the Peace, seizes all Criminals, and sees the Sentences of Justice executed, and whose Authority is like that of a Sheriff in a County with us, or a Constable in a Parish. The *Pensioner*, who is a Civil-Lawyer, verst in the Customs, and Records, and Privileges of the Town, concerning which he informs

the Magistracy upon occasion, and vindicates them upon
disputes with other Towns; He is a Servant of the Senate
and the Burgomasters, delivers their Messages, makes their
Harangues upon all Publick Occasions, and is not unlike the
Recorder in one of our Towns.

In this City of *Amsterdam* is the famous Bank, which is
the greatest Treasure, either real or imaginary, that is
known any where in the World. The place of it is a great
Vault under the Stadthouse, made strong with all the
circumstances of Doors and Locks, and other appearing
cautions of safety, that can be: And 'tis certain, that whoever is carried to see the Bank, shall never fail to find the
appearance of a mighty real Treasure, in Barrs of Gold and
Silver, Plate and infinite Bags of Metals, which are supposed
to be all Gold and Silver, and may be so for ought I know.
But the Burgomasters only having the inspection of this
Bank, and no Man ever taking any particular account of
what issues in and out, from Age to Age, 'tis impossible to
make any calculation, or guess what proportion the real
Treasure may hold to the Credit of it. Therefore the
security of the Bank lies not only in the effects that are in it,
but in the Credit of the whole Town or State of *Amsterdam*,
whose Stock and Revenue is equal to that of some Kingdoms; and who are bound to make good all Moneys that are
brought into their Bank; The Tickets or Bills hereof make
all the usual great Payments, that are made between Man and
Man in the Town; and not only in most other places of the
United Provinces, but in many other Trading-parts of the
World. So as this Bank is properly a general Cash, where
every Man lodges his Money, because he esteems it safer,
and easier paid in and out, than if it were in his Coffers at
home: And the Bank is so far from paying any Interest for

what is there brought in, that Money in the Bank is worth
something more in common Payments, than what runs
current in Coyn from Hand to Hand; No other Money
passing in the Bank, but in the species of Coyn the best
known, the most ascertain'd, and the most generally current
in all parts of the Higher as well as the Lower *Germany*.

The Revenues of *Amsterdam* arise out of the constant
Excise upon all sorts of Commodities bought and sold
within the Precinct: Or, out of the Rents of those Houses or
Lands that belong in common to the City: Or, out of
certain Duties and Impositions upon every House, towards
the uses of Charity, and the Repairs, or Adornments, or
Fortifications, of the place: Or else, out of extraordinary
Levies consented to by the Senate, for furnishing their part
of the Publick Charge that is agreed to by their Deputies in
the Provincial-States, for the use of the Province: Or by the
Deputies of the States of *Holland* in the States-General, for
support of the Union. And all these Payments are made
into one Common Stock of the Town, not, as many of ours
are, into that of the Parish, so as attempts may be easier
made at the calculations of their whole Revenue: And I have
heard it affirmed, That what is paid of all kinds to Publick
Uses of the States-General, the Province, and the City in
Amsterdam, amounts to above Sixteen hundred thousand
pounds *Sterling* a year. But I enter into no Computations,
nor give these for any thing more, than what I have heard
from Men who pretended to make such Enquiries, which,
I confess, I did not. 'Tis certain, that, in no Town, Strength,
Beauty, and Convenience, are better provided for, nor with
more unlimited Expence, than in this, by the Magnificence
of their Publick Buildings, as Stadthouse and Arsenals;
The Number and Spaciousness, as well as Order and

Revenues of their many Hospitals; The commodiousness of their Canals, running through the chief Streets of passage; The mighty strength of their Bastions and Ramparts; And the neatness, as well as convenience, of their Streets, so far as can be compassed in so great a confluence of industrious People: All which could never be atchieved without a Charge much exceeding what seems proportioned to the Revenue of one single Town.

The Senate chuses the Deputies, which are sent from this City to the States of *Holland*[1]; The Soveraignty whereof is represented by Deputies of the Nobles and Towns, composing Nineteen Voices; Of which the Nobles have only the first, and the Cities eighteen, according to the number of those which are called *Stemms*; The other Cities and Towns of the Province having no voice in the States. These Cities were originally but Six, *Dort, Haerlem, Delf, Leyden, Amsterdam*, and *Tergou*. But were encreased by Prince *William* of *Nassaw*, to the number of Eighteen, by the addition of *Rotterdam, Gorcum, Schedam, Schonoven, Briel, Alcmaer, Horne, Enchusen, Edam, Moninckdam, Medenblick*, and *Permeren*. This makes as great an inequality in the Government of the Province, by such a small City as *Permeren* having an equal voice in the Provincial-States with *Amsterdam*, (which pays perhaps half of all charges of the Province,) as seems to be in the States-General by so small a Province as *Overyssel* having an equal voice in the States-General, with that of *Holland*, which contributes more than half to the general charge of the Union. But this was by some Writers of that Age interpreted to be done by the Prince's Authority, to lessen that of the Nobles, and balance that of the greater Cities, by the voices of the

[1] Government of the Province of *Holland*.

smaller, whose dependences were easier to be gained and secured.

The Nobles, though they are few in this Province, yet are not represented by all their number, but by Eight or Nine, who as Deputies from their Body have Session in the States-Provincial; and who, when one among them dyes, chuse another to succeed him. Though they have all together but one voice equal to the smallest Town; yet they are very considerable in the Government, by possessing many of the best Charges both Civil and Military, by having the direction of all the Ecclesiastical Revenue that was seized by the State upon the change of Religion; and by sending their Deputies to all the Councils both of the Generalty and the Province, and by the nomination of one Counsellor in the two great Courts of Justice. They give their Voice first in the Assembly of the States, and thereby a great weight to the business in consultation. The Pensioner of *Holland* is seated with them, delivers their Voice for them, and assists at all their Deliberations, before they come to the Assembly. He is, properly, but Minister or Servant of the Province, and so his Place or Rank is behind all their Deputies; but has always great Credit, because he is perpetual, or seldom discharged; though of right he ought to be chosen or renewed every fifth year. He has place in all the several Assemblies of the Province, and in the States proposes all Affairs, gathers the Opinions, and forms or digests the Resolutions; pretending likewise a Power, not to conclude any very important Affair by plurality of Voices, when he judges in his Conscience he ought not to do it, and that it will be of ill consequence or prejudice to the Province. He is likewise one of their constant Deputies in the States General.

The Deputies of the Cities are drawn out of the Magistrates and Senate of each Town: Their Number is uncertain and Arbitrary, according to the Customs or Pleasure of the Cities that send them, because they have all together but one Voice, and are all maintained at their Cities charge: But commonly one of the Burgomasters, and the Pensioner are of the number.

The States of *Holland* have their Session in the Court at the *Hague*, and assemble ordinarily four times a year, in *February*, *June*, *September*, and *November*. In the former Sessions, they provide for the filling up of all vacant Charges, and for renewing the Farms of all the several Taxes, and for consulting about any matters that concern either the general good of the Province, or any particular differences arising between the Towns. But in *November*, they meet purposely to resolve upon the continuance of the Charge which falls to the share of their Province the following year, according to what may have been agreed upon by the Deputies of the States-General, as necessary for the support of the State or Union.

For extraordinary occasions, they are convoked by a Council called the *Gecommitteerde Raeden*, or the Commissioned Counsellors, who are properly a Council of State, of the Province, composed of several Deputies; One from the Nobles; One from each of the chief Towns; And but One from three of the smaller Towns, each of the three chusing him by turns. And this Council sits constantly at the *Hague*, and both proposes to the Provincial-States, at their extraordinary Assemblies, the matters of deliberation; and executes their Resolutions.

In these Assemblies, though all are equal in Voices, and any one hinders a result; yet it seldom happens, but that united by one common bond of Interest, and having all one common End of Publick Good; They come after full Debates to easie Resolutions; yeilding to the power of Reason, where it is clear and strong; And suppressing all private Passions or Interests, so as the smaller part seldom contests hard or long, what the greater agrees of. When the Deputies of the States agree in Opinion, they send some of their number to their respective Towns, proposing the Affair and the Reasons alledged, and desiring Orders from them to conclude; Which seldom fails, if the necessity or utility be evident: If it be more intricate, or suffers delay, The States adjourn for such a time, as admits the return of all the Deputies to their Towns; where their influence and interest, and the impressions of the Debates in their Provincial Assemblies, make the consent of the Cities easier gain'd.

Besides the States and Council mention'd, the Province has likewise a Chamber of Accounts, who manage the general Revenues of the Province: And, besides this Trust, they have the absolute disposition of the ancient Demesn of *Holland*, without giving any account to the States of the Province. Only at times, either upon usual intervals, or upon a necessity of Money, the States call upon them for a Subsidy of Two or Three Hundred Thousand Crowns, or more, as they are prest, or conceive the Chamber to be grown rich, beyond what is proportioned to the general design of encreasing the ease and fortunes of those Persons who compose it. The States of *Holland* dispose of these charges to Men grown aged in their service, and who have passed through most of the Employments of State, with the esteem of Prudence and Integrity; and such persons find here an honourable and profitable retreat.

The Provinces of *Holland* and *Zealand*, as they used formerly to have one Governour in the time of the House of *Burgundy* and *Austria*; so they have long had one common Judicature, which is exercised by two Courts of Justice, each of them common to both the Provinces. The first is composed of Twelve Counsellors, Nine of *Holland*, and Three of *Zealand*, of whom the Governor of the Provinces is the Head; by the old Constitution used to preside whenever he pleased, and to name all the Counsellors except one, who was chosen by the Nobles. This Court judges without appeal in all Criminal Causes; but in Civil, there lyes appeal to the other Court, which is called the High Council, from which there is no Appeal, but only by Petition to the States of the Province for a revision: When these judge there is reason for it, they grant Letters-Patents to that purpose, naming some *Syndiques* out of the Towns, who being added to the Counsellors of the two former Courts, revise and judge the Cause in the last resort. And this course seems to have been instituted by way of supply or imitation of the Chamber of *Mechlyn*, to which, before the Revolt of the Provinces, there lay an Appeal, by way of Revision, from all or most of the Provincial Courts of Justice, as there still doth in the *Spanish* Provinces of the *Netherlands*.

The Union is made up of the Seven Soveraign Provinces[1] before named, who chuse their respective Deputies, and send them to the *Hague*, for the composing of three several Colledges, called, The States-General, The Council of State, and the Chamber of Accounts. The Soveraign Power of this United-State lyes effectively in the Assembly of the States-General, which used at first to be convoked upon extraordinary occasions, by the Council of State; but that

[1] Government of the *United Provinces*.

seldom, in regard they usually consisted of above Eight hundred Persons, whose meeting together in one place, from so many several parts, gave too great a shake to the whole Body of the Union; made the Debates long, and sometimes confused; the Resolutions slow, and, upon sudden occasions, out of time. In the absence of the States-General, the Council of State represented their Authority, and executed their Resolutions, and judged of the necessity of a new Convocation: Till after the Earl of *Leicester's* departure from the Government, the Provincial-States desired of the General, That they might, by their constant respective Deputies, continue their Assemblies under the Name of *States-General*, which were never after assembled but at *Bergen ap Zoom*, for ratifying, with more solemn form and Authority, the Truce concluded with Duke *Albert* and *Spain*.

This desire of the Provinces was grounded upon the pretences, That the Council of State convoked them but seldom, and at will; and that being to execute all in their absence, they thereby arrogated to themselves too great an Authority in the State. But a more secret reason had greater weight in this Affair, which was, That the *English* Ambassador had, by agreement with Queen *Elizabeth*, a constant place in their Council of State; And upon the distasts arising between the Provinces and the Earl of *Leicester*, with some jealousies of the Queen's disposition to make a Peace with *Spain*, They had no mind that Her Ambassador should be present any longer in the first digestion of their Affairs which was then usually made in the Council of State. And hereupon they first framed the ordinary Council, called the *States-General*, which has ever since passed by that Name, and sits constantly in the

Court at the *Hague*, represents the Soveraignty of the Union, gives Audience and Dispatches to all Foreign Ministers; but yet is indeed only a representative of the States-General, the Assemblies whereof are wholly disused.

The Council of State, the Admiralty, and the Treasury are all subordinate to this Council; All which are continued in as near a resemblance, as could be, to the several Councils used in the time when the Provinces were subject to their several Principalities; or united under One in the Houses of *Burgundy* and *Austria*: Only the several Deputies (composing one voice) now succeeding the single Persons employed under the former Governments: And the *Hague*, which was the ancient Seat of the Counts of *Holland*, still continues to be so of all these Councils; where the Palace of the former Soveraigns lodges the Prince of *Orange* as Governour, and receives these several Councils as attending still upon the Soveraignty, represented by the States-General.

The Members of all these Councils are placed and changed by the several Provinces, according to their different or agreeing Customs. To the States-General every one sends their Deputies, in what number they please; some Two, some Ten or Twelve; Which makes no difference, because all matters are carried, not by the Votes of Persons, but of Provinces; and all the Deputies from one Province, how few or many soever, have one single Vote. The Provinces differ likewise in the time fixed for their Deputation; some sending for a Year, some for more, and others for life. The Province of *Holland*, send to the States-General one of their Nobles, who is perpetual; Two Deputies chosen out of their Eight chief Towns; and One out of *North-Holland*; and with these, Two of their Provincial Council of State, and their *Pensioner*.

Neither Stadtholder or Governour, or any person in Military charge, has Session in the States-General. Every Province presides their week in turns, and by the most qualified Person of the Deputies of that Province: He sits in a Chair with Arms, at the middle of a long Table, capable of holding about Thirty Persons; For about that number this Council is usually composed of. The *Greffier*, who is in nature of a Secretary, sits at the lower end of the Table: When a Foreign Minister has Audience, he is seated at the middle of this Table, over against the President: Who proposes all matters in this Assembly; Makes the *Greffier* read all Papers; Puts the Question; Calls the Voices of the Provinces; And forms the Conclusion. Or, if he refuses to conclude according to the plurality, he is obliged to resign his Place to the President of the ensuing week, who concludes for him.

This is the course in all Affairs before them, except in cases of Peace and War, of Foreign Alliances, of Raising, or Coining, of Monies, or the Priviledges of each Province or Member of the Union. In all which, All the Provinces must concur, Plurality being not at all weighed or observed. This Council is not Soveraign, but only represents the Soveraignty; and therefore, though Ambassadors are both received and sent in their Name; yet neither are their own chosen, nor Foreign Ministers answered, nor any of those mentioned Affairs resolved, without consulting first the States of each Province by their respective Deputies, and receiving Orders from them; And in other important Matters, though decided by Plurality, They frequently consult with the Council of State.

Nor has this Method or Constitution ever been broken since their State began, excepting only in one Affair, which was in *January* 1668, when His Majesty sent me over to propose a League of Mutual Defence with this State, and another for the preservation of *Flanders* from the invasion of *France*, which had already conquered a great part of the *Spanish* Provinces, and left the rest at the mercy of the next *Campania*. Upon this occasion I had the fortune to prevail with the States-General, to conclude three Treaties, and upon them draw up and sign the several Instruments, in the space of Five days; Without passing the essential Forms of their Government by any recourse to the Provinces, which must likewise have had it to the several Cities; There, I knew, those Foreign Ministers, whose Duty and Interest it was to oppose this Affair, expected to meet, and to elude it, which could not have failed, in case it had run that circle, since engaging the Voice of one City must have broken it. 'Tis true, that in concluding these Alliances without Commission from their Principals, The Deputies of the States-General ventur'd their Heads, if they had been disowned by their Provinces; but being all unanimous, and led by the clear evidence of so direct, and so important an Interest, (which must have been lost by the usual delays,) They all agreed to run the hazard; and were so far from being disowned, that they were applauded by all the Members of every Province; Having thereby changed the whole face of Affairs in Christendom, and laid the foundation of the Triple-Alliance, and the Peace of *Aix*, (which were concluded about Four Months after.) So great has the force of Reason and Interest ever proved in this State, not only to the uniting of all Voices in their Assemblies, but to the absolving of the greatest breach of their Original

Constitutions; Even in a State, whose Safety and Greatness has been chiefly founded upon the severe and exact observance of Order and Method, in all their Counsels and Executions. Nor have they ever used, at any other time, any greater means to agree and unite the several Members of their Union, in the Resolutions necessary, upon the most pressing occasions, than for the agreeing-Provinces to name some of their ablest persons to go and confer with the dissenting, and represent those Reasons and Interests, by which they have been induced to their Opinions.

The Council of State is composed of Deputies from the several Provinces, but after another manner than the States-General, the number being fixed. *Gelderland* sends Two, *Holland* Three, *Zealand* and *Utrecht* Two apiece, *Friezeland*, *Overyssel* and *Groninghen*, each of them One, making in all Twelve. They Vote not by Provinces, but by Personal Voices; and every Deputy presides by turns. In this Council the Governour of the Provinces has Session, and a decisive voice; And the Treasurer-General, Session, but a voice only deliberative; yet he has much credit here, being for life; and so is the person deputed to this Council from the Nobles of *Holland*, and the Deputies of the Province of *Zealand*. The rest are but for two, three, or four years.

The Council of State executes the Resolution of the States-General; consults and proposes to them the most expedient ways of raising Troops, and levying Monies, as well as the proportions of both, which they conceive necessary in all Conjunctures and Revolutions of the State: Superintends the Milice, the Fortifications, the Contributions out of Enemies Country, the forms and disposal of all Passports, and the Affairs, Revenues, and Government of all places conquered since the Union; which, being gain'd by the common Arms of this State, depend upon the States-General, and not upon any particular Province.

Towards the end of every year, this Council forms a state of the Expence they conceive will be necessary for the year ensuing; Presents it to the States-General, desiring them to demand so much of the States-Provincial, to be raised according to the usual Proportions, which are of 100000 G^{rs}.

	g^{rs}	st	d
Gelderland	3612	05	00
Holland	58309	01	10
Zealand	9183	14	02
Utrecht	5830	17	11
Frieʒeland	11661	15	10
Overyssel	3571	08	04
Groningue	5830	17	11

This Petition, as 'tis called, is made to the States-General, in the Name of the Governour and Council of State, which is but a continuance of the forms used in the time of their Soveraigns, and still by the Governors and Council of State in the *Spanish-Netherlands*: Petition signifying barely asking or demanding, though implying the thing demanded to be wholly in the right and power of them that give. It was used by the first Counts, only upon extraordinary occasions, and necessities; but in the time of the Houses of *Burgundy* and *Austria*, grew to be a thing of course, and Annual, as it is still in the *Spanish* Provinces.

The Council of State disposes of all sums of Money destin'd for all extraordinary Affairs, and expedites the Orders for the whole expence of the State, upon the

Resolutions first taken, in the main, by the States-General. The Orders must be Signed by Three Deputies of several Provinces, as well as by the Treasurer-General, and then Registred in the Chamber of Accounts, before the Receiver-General pays them, which is then done without any difficulty, charge, or delay.

Every Province raises what Monies it pleases, and by what ways or means; sends its *Quota*, or share, of the general charge, to the Receiver-General, and converts the rest to the present use, or reserves it for the future occasions, of the Province.

The Chamber of Accounts was erected about Sixty years ago, for the ease of the Council of State, to Examine and state all accounts of all the several Receivers, to Controul and Register the Orders of the Council of State, which disposes of the Finances: And this Chamber is composed of two Deputies from each Province, who are changed every Three years.

Besides these Colledges, is the Council of the Admiralty; who, when the States-General, by Advice of the Council of State, have destin'd a Fleet of such a number and force to be set out, have the absolute disposition of the Marine Affairs, as well in the choice and equipage of all the several Ships, as in issuing the Monies allotted for that Service.

This Colledge is subdivided into Five, of which three are in *Holland*, *viz*. One in *Amsterdam*, another at *Rotterdam*, and the third at *Horn*: The Fourth is at *Middlebourgh* in *Zealand*, and the Fifth at *Harlinguen* in *Friezeland*. Each of these is composed of Seven Deputies, Four of that Province where the Colledge resides; and Three named by the other Provinces. The Admiral, or, in his absence, the Vice-Admiral, has Session in all these Colledges, and presides when he is present. They take cognizance of all Crimes committed at Sea; judge all Pirats that are taken, and all Frauds or Negligences in the payment or collections of the Customs; which are particularly affected to the Admiralty, and appliable to no other use. This *Fond* being not sufficient in times of Wars, is supplied by the States with whatever more is necessary from other *Fonds*; but in time of Peace, being little exhausted by other constant charge, besides that of Convoys to their several Fleets of Merchants in all parts, The remainder of this Revenue is applied to the building of great Ships of War, and furnishing the several Arsenals and Stores with all sorts of Provision, necessary for the Building and Rigging of more Ships than can be needed by the course of a long War.

So soon as the number and force of the Fleets, designed for any Expedition, is agreed by the States-General, and given out by the Council of State to the Admiralty; Each particular Colledg furnishes their own proportion, which is known as well as that of the several Provinces, in all Monies that are to be raised. In all which, the Admiral has no other share or advantages, besides his bare Salary, and his proportion in Prizes that are taken. The Captains and Superior Officers of each Squadron are chosen by the several Colledges; the number of Men appointed for every Ship: After which, each Captain uses his best diligence and credit to fill his number with the best Men he can get, and takes the whole care and charge of Victualling his own Ship for the time intended for that Expedition, and signify'd to him by the Admiralty; and this at a certain rate of so much a Man. And by the good or ill discharge of his Trust, as well as that of providing Chirurgeons Medicines, and all things necessary for the Health of the Men, each Captain grows into good or ill credit with the Seamen, and, by their report, with the Admiralties; Upon whose Opinion and Esteem, the fortune of all Sea-Officers depends: So as, in all their Expeditions, there appears rather an emulation among the particular Captains who shall treat his Seamen best in these points, and employ the Monies, allotted for their Victualling, to the best advantage, than any little Knavish Practices, of filling their own Purses, by keeping their Men's Bellies empty, or forcing them to corrupted un-wholsome Diet: Upon which, and upon cleanliness in their Ships, the health of many People crowded up into so little Rooms, seem chiefly to depend.

The Salaries of all the Great Officers of this State, are very small: I have already mentioned that of a Burgo-master's of *Amsterdam* to be about fifty pounds *sterling* a year: That of their Vice-Admiral (for since the last Prince of *Orange's* death, to the year 1670, there had been no Admiral) is Five hundred, and that of the *Pensioner* of *Holland* Two hundred.

The Greatness of this State seems much to consist in these Orders, how confused soever, and of different pieces, they may seem: But more in two main effects of them, which are, The good choice of the Officers of chief Trust in the Cities, Provinces, and State: And the great simplicity and modesty in the common Port or living of their chiefest Ministers; without which, the Absoluteness of the Senates in each Town, and the Immensity of Taxes throughout the whole State, would never be endured by the People with any patience; being both of them greater than in many of those Governments, which are esteemed most Arbitrary among their Neighbours. But in the Assemblies and De-bates of their Senates, every Man's Abilities are discovered, as their Dispositions are, in the conduct of their Lives and Domestick, among their fellow-Citizens. The observation of these either raises, or suppresses, the credit of particular Men, both among the People, and the Senates of their Towns; who, to maintain their Authority with less popular Envy or Discontent, give much to the general Opinion of the People in the choice of their Magistrates: By this means it comes to pass, that, though perhaps the Nation generally be not wise, yet the Government is, Because it is composed of the wisest of the Nation; which may give it an advantage over many others, where Ability is of more common growth, but of less use to the Publique; if it happens, that neither Wisdom nor Honesty are the Qualities, which bring men to the management of State-Affairs, as they usually do in this Common-wealth.

Besides, though these People, who are naturally Cold and Heavy, may not be ingenious enough to furnish a pleasant or agreeable Conversation, yet they want not plain down-right Sense to understand and do their Business both publick and private, which is a Talent very different from the other; and I know not, whether they often meet: For the First proceeds from heat of the brain, which makes the Spirits more airy and volatile, and thereby the motions of Thought lighter and quicker, and the range of Imagination much greater than in cold Heads, where the Spirits are more earthy and dull; Thought moves slower and heavier, but thereby the impressions of it are deeper, and last longer: One Imagination being not so frequently, nor so easily, effaced by another, as where new ones are continually arising. This makes duller Men more constant and steddy, and quicker Men more inconstant and uncertain: whereas the greatest ability in business seems to be the steddy persuit of some one thing, till there is an end of it, with perpetual application and endeavour not to be diverted by every representation of new hopes or fears of difficulty, or danger, or of some better design. The first of these Talents cuts like a Razor, the other like a Hatchet: One has thinness of edg, and fineness of metal and temper, but is easily turn'd by any substance that is hard, and resists. T'other has toughness and weight, which makes it cut thorough, or go deep, wherever it falls; and therefore one is for Adornment, and t'other for Use.

It may be said further, that the heat of the Heart commonly goes along with that of the Brain; so that Passions are warmer, where Imaginations are quicker: And there are few Men, (unless in case of some evident natural defect) but have sense enough to distinguish in gross between right and wrong, between Good and Bad, when represented to them; and consequently have judgment enough to do their business, if it be left to itself, and not swayed nor corrupted by some Humour or Passion, by Anger or Pride, by Love or by Scorn, Ambition or Avarice, Delight or Revenge; so that the coldness of Passions seems to be the natural ground of Ability and Honesty among Men, as the Government or Moderation of them the great End of Philosophical and Moral Instructions. These Speculations may perhaps a little lessen the common wonder, How we should meet with in one Nation so little show of Parts, and of Wit, and so great evidence of Wisdom and Prudence, as has appeared in the Conduct and Successes of this State, for near an Hundred Years; Which needs no other testimony, than the mighty growth and Power it arrived to, from so weak and contemptible Seeds and Beginnings.

The other Circumstance, I mentioned, as an occasion of

their Greatness, was, the simplicity and modesty of their Magistrates in their way of Living; which is so general, that I never knew One among them exceed the common frugal popular Air; And so great, That of the Two chief Officers in my time, Vice-Admiral *De Ruiter*, and the Pensioner *De Wit*; (One, generally esteemed by Foreign Nations, as great a Seaman; and the other, as great a States-man, as any of their Age,) I never saw the first in Cloaths better than the commonest Sea-Captain, nor with above one Man following him, nor in a Coach: And in his own House, neither was the Size, Building, Furniture, or Entertainment, at all exceeding the use of every common Merchant and Tradesman in his Town. For the Pensioner *De Wit*, who had the great influence in the Government, The whole Train and Expence of his Domestique went very equal with other common Deputies or Ministers of the State; His Habit grave, and plain, and popular; His Table, what only serv'd turn for his Family, or a Friend; His Train (besides Commissaries and Clerks kept for him in an Office adjoyning to his House, at the publique charge,) was only one Man, who performed all the Menial service of his House at home; and upon his Visits of Ceremony, putting on a plain Livery-Cloak, attended his Coach abroad: For upon other occasions, He was seen usually in the streets on foot and alone, like the commonest Burger of the Town. Nor was this manner of life affected, or used only by these particular Men, but was the general fashion or mode among all the Magistrates of the State: For I speak not of the Military Officers, who are reckon'd their Servants, and live in a different garb, though generally modester than in other Countries.

Thus this stomachful People, who could not endure the

least exercise of Arbitrary Power or Impositions, or the
sight of any Foreign Troops under the *Spanish* Government; Have been since inured to all of them, in the highest
degree, under their own popular Magistrates; Bridled with
hard Laws; Terrified with severe Executions; Environ'd
with Foreign Forces; And opprest with the most cruel
Hardship and variety of Taxes, that was ever known under
any Government. But all this, whilst the way to Office and
Authority lies through those qualities, which acquire the
general esteem of the People; Whilst no Man is exempted
from the danger and current of Laws; Whilst Soldiers are
confin'd to Frontier-Garisons, (the Guard of Inland, or
Trading, Towns being left to the Burghers themselves;)
And whilst no great Riches are seen to enter by Publique
Payments into private Purses, either to raise Families, or to
feed the prodigal Expences of vain, extravagant, and lux-
urious Men; But all Publique Monies are applied to the
Safety, Greatness, or Honour of the State, and the Magistrates themselves bear an equal share in all the Burthens,
they impose.

The Authority of the Princes of *Orange*[1], though inter-
mitted upon the untimely death of the last, and infancy of
this present, Prince; Yet, as it must be ever acknowledged
to have had a most essential part in the first frame of this
Government, and in all the Fortunes thereof, during the
whole growth and progress of the State: So, has it ever
preserved a very strong root, not only in Six of the Provinces, but even in the general and popular affections of the
Province of *Holland* it self, Whose States have for these
last Twenty years so much endeavoured to suppress, or
exclude, it.

[1] The Authority of the Princes of *Orange*.

This began in the Person of Prince *William* of *Nassaw*, at the very birth of the State; And not so much by the Quality of being Governour of *Holland* and *Zealand* in *Charles* the Fifth's, and *Philip* the Second's time; As by the esteem of so great Wisdom, Goodness and Courage, as excell'd in that Prince, and seems to have been from him derived to his whole Race, being, indeed, the qualities that naturally acquire Esteem and Authority among the People, in all Governments. Nor has this Nation in particular, since the time perhaps of *Civilis*, ever been without some Head, under some Title or other; but always an Head subordinate to their Laws and Customs, and to the Soveraign Power of the State.

In the first Constitution of this Government, after the Revolt from *Spain*, All the Power and Rights of Prince *William* of *Orange*, as Governour of the Provinces, seem to have been carefully reserved. But those which remain'd inherent in the Soveraign, were devolved upon the Assembly of the States-General, so as in them remained the power of making Peace and War, and all Foreign Alliances, and of raising and coining of Monies. In the Prince, the Command of all Land and Sea-Forces, as Captain-General and Admiral, and thereby the disposition of all Military Commands; The Power of pardoning the Penalty of Crimes; The chusing of Magistrates upon the nomination of the Towns; For they presented three to the Prince, who elected one out of that number. Originally the States-General were convoked by the Council of State, where the Prince had the greatest influence: Nor, since that change, have the States used to resolve any important matter without his advice. Besides all this, As the States-General represented the Soveraignty, so did the Prince of *Orange*

the Dignity, of this State, by publique Guards, and the
attendance of all Military Officers; By the application of all
Foreign Ministers, and all pretenders at home; By the
Splendor of his Court, and Magnificence of his Expence,
supported not only by the Pensions and Rights of his
several Charges and Commands, but by a mighty Patrimonial Revenue in Lands and Soveraign Principalities, and
Lordships, as well in *France*, *Germany*, and *Burgundy*, as in
the several parts of the Seventeen Provinces; so as Prince
Henry was used to answer some, that would have flatter'd
him into the designs of a more Arbitrary Power, That he
had as much as any wise Prince would desire in that State;
since he wanted none indeed, besides that of Punishing
Men, and raising Money; whereas he had rather the envy of
the first should lye upon the Forms of the Government;
and he knew the other could never be supported without
the consent of the People, to that degree which was necessary for the defence of so small a State, against so mighty
Princes as their Neighbors.

Upon these Foundations was this State first establisht,
and by these Orders maintained, till the death of the last
Prince of *Orange*; When, by the great influence of the
Province of *Holland* amongst the rest, the Authority of the
Princes came to be shared among the several Magistracies
of the State; Those of the Cities assumed the last nomination of their several Magistrates; The States-Provincial, the
disposal of all Military Commands in those Troops, which
their share was to pay; And the States-General, the Command of the Armies, by Officers of their own appointment,
substituted and changed at their Will. No power remain'd
to pardon what was once condemned by rigor of Law; Nor
any Person to represent the Port and Dignity of a Sove-

raign State; Both which could not fail of being sensibly missed by the People; since no Man in particular can be secure of offending, or would therefore absolutely despair of impunity himself, though he would have others do so; And Men are generally pleased with the Pomp and Splendor of a Government, not only as it is an amusement for idle People, but, as it is a mark of the Greatness, Honour and Riches, of their Country.

However, these Defects were for near Twenty years supplied in some measure, and this Frame supported by the great Authority and Riches of the Province of *Holland*, which drew a sort of dependence from the other Six; and by the great Sufficiency, Integrity, and Constancy of their chief Minister, and by the effect of both in the prosperous Successes of their Affairs: Yet having been a Constitution strained against the current vein and humour of the People; It was always evident, that upon the growth of this young Prince, The great Virtues and Qualities he derived from the mixture of such Royal and such Princely Blood, could not fail in time of raising His Authority to equal, at least, if not to surpass that of his Glorious Ancestors.

Because the curious may desire to know somthing of the other Provinces, as well as *Holland*, at least, in general, and where they differ; It may be observed, That the Constitutions of *Gelderland, Zealand,* and *Utrecht,* agree much with those of *Holland*; the States in each Province being composed of Deputies from the Nobles and the Cities; But with these small differences; In *Gelderland,* all the Nobles, that have certain Fees, or Lordships, in the Province, have Session, they compose one half of the States, and the Deputies of the Towns the other; and though some certain persons among them are deputed to the States-General; Yet any of the Nobles of *Gelder* may have place there, if he will attend at his own charge.

In *Zealand*, the Nobility having been extinguished in the *Spanish* Wars; And the Prince of *Orange* possessing the Marquisats of *Flushing* and *Terveer*, His Highness alone makes that part of the States in the Province, by the Quality and Title of First, or Sole, Noble of *Zealand*; And thereby has, by his Deputy, the first Place, and Voice, in the States of the Province, the Council of State, and Chamber of Accounts: As Soveraign of *Flushing* and *Terveer*, he likewise creates the Magistrates, and consequently disposes the Voices, not only of the Nobles, but also of Two Towns, whereas there are in all but Six, that send their Deputies to the States, and make up the Soveraignty of the Province.

In *Utrecht*, besides the Deputies of the Nobles, and Towns, Eight Delegates of the Clergy have Session, and make a third Member in the States of the Province. These are elected out of the four great Chapters of the Town, the Preferments and Revenues whereof, (though anciently Ecclesiastical) yet are now possessed by Lay-persons, who are most of them Gentlemen of the Province.

The Government of the Province of *Friezland* is wholly different from that of the Four Provinces already mentioned; And is composed of Four Members, which are called, The quarter of *Ostergo*, consisting of Eleven Baillages; Of *Westergo*, consisting of Nine; and of *Seveawolden*, consisting of Ten. Each Baillage comprehends a certain number of Villages, Ten, Twelve, Fifteen, or Twenty, according to their several extents. The Fourth Member consists of the Towns of the Province, which are Eleven in number. These Four Members have each of them right of sending their Deputies to the States, that is, Two chosen out of every Baillage, and Two out of every Town, And these represent the Soveraignty of the Province, and deliberate and conclude of all Affairs, of what importance soever, without any recourse to those who deputed them, or obligation to know their intentions, which the Deputies of all the former Provinces are strictly bound to, and either must follow the Instructions they bring with them to the Assembly, or know the resolution of their Principals before they conclude of any new Affair, that arises.

In the other Provinces, the Nobles of the Towns chuse the Deputies which compose the States, but in *Friezland* the Constitution is of quite another sort. For every Baillage, which is composed of a certain extent of Country, and number of Villages, (as has been said) is Governed by a Bailly, whom in their Language they call *Greetman*, and this Officer Governs his Circuit with the assistance of a certain number of persons, who are called his Assessors, who, together, judge of all Civil Causes, in the first instance, but with appeal to the Court of Justice of the Province. When the States are convoked, every Bailly assembles together all the persons of what quality soever, who possess a certain quantity of Land within his district, and these Men, by most voices, name the Two Deputies which each Baillage sends to the Assembly of the States.

This Assembly, as it represents the Soveraignty of the Province; so it disposes of all vacant charges, chuses the Nine Deputies, who compose that permanent Colledge, which is the Council of State of the Province; And likewise Twelve Counsellors, (that is, Three for every Quarter) who compose the Court of Justice of the Province, and Judge of all Civil Causes in the last resort, but of all Criminal from the first instance. There being no other Criminal Jurisdic-

tion, but this only through the Province; Whereas, in the
other Provinces, there is no Town which has it not within
itself; And several, both Lords, and Villages, have the
High and Low Justice belonging to them.

In the Province of *Groningue* which is upon the same
Tract of Land, the Elections of the Deputies out of the
Country are made as in *Friezland*, by persons possest of set
proportions of Land; But in *Overyssel*, All Nobles who are
qualify'd by having Seigneurial Lands make a part of the
States.

These three Provinces, with *Westphalia*, and all those
Countries between the *Wezer*, the *Yssell*, and the *Rhyne*,
were the Seat of the ancient *Frisons*, who, under the name of
Saxons, (given them from the weapon they wore, made like
a Sithe, with the edge outwards, and called in their Lan-
guage *Seaxes*) were the fierce Conquerors of our *British*
Island, being called in upon the desertion of the *Roman*
Forces, and the cruel incursions of the *Picts* against a
People, whose long Wars, at first with the *Romans*, and
afterwards Servitude under them, had exhausted all the
bravest Blood of their Nation, either in their own, or their
Masters, succeeding quarrels, and depressed the Hearts and
Courages of the rest.

The Bishop of *Munster*, whose Territories lye in this
Tract of Land, gave me the first certain evidences of those
being the Seats of our ancient *Saxons*, which have since
been confirmed to me by many things I have observed in
reading the Stories of those times, and by what has been
affirmed to me upon enquiry of the *Friezons* old Language,
having still so great affinity with our old *English*, as to
appear easily to have been the same; most of their words
still retaining the same signification and sound; very

different from the Language of the *Hollanders*. This is the most remarkable in a little Town called *Malcuera*, upon the *Zudder* Sea, in *Friezland*, which is still built after the fashion of the old *German* Villages, described by *Tacitus*; without any use or observation of Lines or Angles; but as if every Man had built in a common Field, just where he had a mind, so as a stranger, when he goes in, must have a Guide to find the way out again.

Upon these Informations, and Remarques, and the particular account afterwards given me of the Constitutions of the Province of *Friezland*, so different from the others; I began to make reflections upon them, as the likeliest Originals of many ancient Constitutions among us, of which, no others can be found, and which may seem to have been introduced by the *Saxons* here, and by their long and absolute possession of that part of the Isle, called *England*, to have been so planted and rooted among us, as to have waded safe, in a great measure, through the succeeding inundations and conquests of the *Danish* and *Norman* Nations. And, perhaps, there may be much matter found for the curious remarks of some diligent, and studious Antiquaries, in the comparisons of the *Bailli*, or *Greetman* among the *Frisons*, with our *Sheriffe*: Of their *Assessors*, with our *Justices* of Peace: Of their Judging Civil Causes in their district, upon the first resort, but not without appeal, with the course of our Quarter-Sessions: Of their chief Judicature, being composed of Counsellors, of four several Quarters, with our four Circuits: Of these being the common Criminal Judicature of the Country: Of the Composition of their States, with our Parliament, at least, our House of Commons: In the particulars of Two Deputies, being chosen from each Town, as with us, and

two from each Baillage, as from each County here; And
these last by Voices of all persons, possest of a certain
quantity of Land; And at a Meeting assembled by the
Greetman to that purpose; And these Deputies having
power to resolve of all matters without resort to those that
chose them, or knowledge of their intentions, which are all
circumstances agreeing with our Constitutions, but absolutely differing from those of the other Provinces in the
United States, and from the composition, I think, of the
States, either now, or formerly, used in the other Nations
of *Europe.*

To this Original, I suppose, we likewise owe what I have
often wondred at, that in *England* we neither see, nor find
upon record, any Lord, or Lordship, that pretends to have
the exercise of Judicature belong to it, either that which is
called High, or Low, Justice, which seems to be a Badge of
some ancient Soveraignty, Though we see them very
frequent among our Neighbours, both under more arbitrary
Monarchies, and under the most free and popular States.

CHAPTER III

Of their Scituation

*H*olland, *Zealand*, *Friezland* and *Groninguen*, are seated upon the Sea, and make the Strength and Greatness of this State: The other three, with the conquered Towns in *Brabant*, *Flanders*, and *Cleve*, make only the Outworks or Frontiers, serving chiefly for Safety and Defence of these. No Man can tell the strange and mighty Changes, that may have been made in the Face and Bounds of Maritime Countries, at one time or other, by furious Inundations, upon the unusual concurrence of Land-Floods, Winds, and Tides; And therefore no Man knows, whether the Province of *Holland* may not have been, in some past Ages, all Wood, and rough unequal Ground, as some old Traditions go; And levell'd to what we see, by the Seas breaking in, and continuing long, upon the Land; since, recovered by its recess, and with the help of Industry. For it is evident, that the Sea for some space of years, advances continually upon one Coast, retiring from the opposite; and in another Age, quite changes this course, yielding up what it had seized, and seizing what it had yielded up, without any reason to be given of such contrary motions. But, I suppose, this great change was made in *Holland*, when the Sea first parted *England* from the Continent, breaking through a neck of Land between *Dover* and *Calais*; Which may be a Tale, but I am sure is no Record. It is certain, on the contrary, that Sixteen hundred years ago, there was no usual Mention or Memory of any such Changes; and that the face of all these Coasts, and nature of the Soil, especially that of *Holland*, was much as it is now, allowing only the Improvements of Riches, Time, and Industry; which appears by the description made in *Tacitus*, both of the limits of the Isle of *Batavia*, and the nature of the Soil, as well as the Climate, with the very Names, and course of Rivers, still remaining[1].

'Tis likely, the Changes, arrived since that Age in these Countries, may have been made by stoppages grown in time, with the rolling of Sands upon the mouths of three great Rivers, which disimbogued into the Sea through the Coasts of these Provinces; That is, the *Rhine*, the *Mose*, and the *Scheld*. The ancient *Rhine* divided, where *Skencksconce* now stands, into two Rivers; of which, one kept the name, till, running near *Leyden*, it fell into the Sea at *Catwick*; where are still seen, at low Tides, the Foundations of an ancient *Roman* Castle that commanded the mouth of this River: But this is wholly stopt up, though a great Canal still preserves the Name of the *Old Rhine*. The *Mose*, running by *Dort* and *Rotterdam*, fell, as it now does, into the Sea at the *Briel*, with mighty issues of Water; But the Sands, gather'd for three or four Leagues upon this Coast, make the Haven extreme dangerous, without great skill of Pilots, and use of Pilot-boats, that come out with every Tide, to welcome and secure the Ships bound for that River; And it is probable, that these Sands, having obstructed the free course of the River has at times caused or encreased those Inundations, out of which so many Islands have been recovered, and of which, that part of the Country is so much composed.

---

[1] Rhenus apud principium agri Batavi velut in duos amnes dividitur, ad Gallicam ripam latior & placidior verso cognomento Vahalem accolae dicunt, mox id quoque vocabulum mutat Mosâ flumine, ejusq; immenso ore eundem in Oceanum effunditur.

Cum interim flexu Autumni & crebris imbribus superfusus amnis palustrem humilemq; Insulam in faciem Stagni opplevit.

The *Scheld* seems to have had its issue by *Walcheren* in *Zealand*, which was an Island in the mouth of that River, till the Inundations of that, and the *Mose*, seem to have been joyned together, by some great Helps, or Irruptions of the Sea, by which, the whole Country was overwhelmed, which now makes that Inland-Sea, that serves for a common passage between *Holland*, *Zealand*, *Flanders*, and *Brabant*; The Sea, for some Leagues from *Zealand*, lyes generally upon such Banks of Sand, as it does upon the mouth of the *Maʒe*, though separated by something better Channels than are found in the other.

That which seems likeliest to have been the occasion of stopping up wholly one of these Rivers, and obstructing the others, Is the course of Westerly Winds, (which drive upon this Shore) being so much more constant and violent than the East: For, taking the Seasons, and Years, one with another, I suppose, there will be observed three parts of Westerly for one of Easterly Winds; Besides, that these generally attend the calm Frosts and fair weather; and the other, the stormy and foul. And I have had occasion to make experiment of the Sands rising and sinking before a Haven, by two Fits of these contrary Winds, above four Foot. This, I presume, is likewise the natural reason of so many deep and commodious Havens found upon all the *English* side of the Channel, and so few, (or indeed none) upon the *French* and *Dutch*: An advantage seeming to be given us by Nature, and never to be equall'd by any Art, or Expence, of our Neighbours.

I remember no mention in ancient Authors of that, which is now call'd the *Zudder-Sea*; Which makes me imagine, That may have been form'd likewise by some great Inundation, breaking in between the *Tessel*-Islands, and

others, that lye still in a line contiguous, and like the
broken remainders of a continued Coast. This seems more
probable, from the great shallowness of that Sea, and
flatness of the Sands, upon the whole extent of it; From
the violent rage of the Waters breaking in that way, which
threaten the parts of *North-Holland* about *Medenblick* and
Enchusen, and brave it over the highest and strongest
Digues of the Province, upon every High Tide, and Storm
at North-west. As likewise from the Names of *East* and
West-Friezland, which should have been one Continent,
till divided by this Sea: For, in the time of *Tacitus*, no other
distinction was known, but that of Greater or Lesser
Frisons, and that only from the measure of their numbers, or
forces; and though they were said to have great Lakes
among them, yet that Word seems to import they were of
fresh Water, which is made yet plainer by the Word
Ambiunt [1], that shews those Lakes to have been inhabited
round by these Nations; From all this I should guess, that
the more Inland part of the *Zudder* Sea, was one of the
Lakes there mention'd, between which and the *Tessell* and
Ulie Islands, there lay anciently a great Tract of Land,
(where the Sands are still so shallow, and so continued, as
seems to make it evident:) But since covered by some
great irruptions of Waters, that joyned those of the Sea,
and the Lake together, and thereby made that great Bay,
now called the *Zudder Sea*, by favour whereof, the Town of
Amsterdam has grown to be the most frequented Haven of
the World.

Whatever it was, whether Nature or Accident, and upon

[1] A fronte Frisii excipiunt Majoribus Minoribusque Frisiis vocabulum,
ex modo virium utraeque Nationes usque ad Oceanum Rheno praetex-
untur *ambiuntq; immensos insuper lacus. *Tacit. de Mor. Ger.*

what occasion soever it arrived, The Soil of the whole
Province of *Holland* is generally flat, like the Sea in a calm,
and looks as if after a long contention between Land and
Water, which It should belong to, It had at length been
divided between them: For to consider the great Rivers,
and the strange number of Canals that are found in this
Province, and do not only lead to every great Town, but
almost to every Village, and every Farm-House in the
Country; And the infinity of Sails that are seen every where
coursing up and down upon them; One would imagine the
Water to have shar'd with the Land; and the People that
live in Boats, to hold some proportion with those that live
in Houses. And this is one great advantage towards Trade,
which is natural to the Scituation, and not to be attained in
any Country, where there is not the same level and softness
of Soil, which makes the cutting of Canals so easie work, as
to be attempted almost by every private Man; And one
Horse shall draw in a Boat more than fifty can do by Cart,
whereas Carriage makes a great part of the price in all
heavy Commodities: And by this easie way of Travelling,
an industrious Man loses no time from his Business, for he
Writes, or Eats, or Sleeps, while he goes; whereas the
Time of Labouring or industrious Men, is the greatest
Native Commodity of any Country.

There is, besides, one very great Lake of fresh Water still
remaining in the midst of this Province, by the name of
Harlem Maer, which might, as they say, be easily drained,
and would thereby make a mighty addition of Land to a
Country, where nothing is more wanted; and receive a
great quantity of People, in which they abound, and who
make their Greatness and Riches. Much Discourse there
has been about such an Attempt, but the City of *Leyden*

having no other way of refreshing their Town, or renewing the water of their Canals, but from this *Maer*, will never consent to it. On the other side, *Amsterdam* will ever oppose the opening and cleansing of the old Channel of the *Rhine*, which they say, might easily be compassed, and by which, the Town of *Leyden* would grow Maritime, and share a great part of the Trade now engrossed by *Amsterdam*. There is in *North-Holland* an Essay already made, at the possibility of draining these great Lakes, by one, of about two Leagues broad, having been made firm Land, within these Forty years; This makes that part of the Country called the *Bemster*, being now the richest Soil of the Province, lying upon a dead flat, divided with Canals, and the ways through it distinguisht with ranges of Trees, which make the pleasantest Summer-Landschip of any Country I have seen, of that sort.

Another advantage of their Scituation of Trade, is made by those Two great Rivers of the *Rhyne* and *Mose*, reaching up, and Navigable, so mighty a length, into so rich and populous Countries of the Higher and Lower *Germany*; which as it brings down all the Commodities from those parts to the Magazines in *Holland*, that vent them by their Shipping into all parts of the World, where the Market calls for them; so, with something more Labour and Time, it returns all the Merchandizes of other parts, into those Countries, that are seated upon these Streams. For their commodious Seat, as to the Trade of the *Streights*, or ·*Baltique*, or any parts of the Ocean, I see no advantage they have of most parts of *England*; and they must certainly yield to many we possess, if we had other equal circumstances to value them.

The lowness and flatness of their Lands, makes in a great

measure the richness of their Soil, that is easily overflowed every Winter, so as the whole Country, at that season, seems to lye under Water, which, in Spring, is driven out again by Mills. But that which mends the Earth, spoils the Air, which would be all Fog and Mist, if it were not clear'd by the sharpness of their Frosts, which never fail with every East Wind for about four Months of the year, and are much fiercer than in the same Latitude with us, because that Wind comes to them over a mighty length of dry Continent; but is moistned by the Vapours, or softned by the warmth of the Seas motion, before it reaches us.

And this is the greatest disadvantage of Trade they receive from their Scituation, though necessary to their Health; because many times their Havens are all shut up for two or three Months with Ice, when ours are open and free.

The fierce sharpness of these Winds makes the changes of their Weather and Seasons more violent and surprising, than in any place I know; so as a warm faint Air turns in a night to a sharp Frost, with the Wind coming into the North-East; And the contrary with another change of Wind. The Spring is much shorter, and less agreeable, than with us; the Winter much colder, and some parts of the Summer much hotter; and I have known more than once, the violence of one give way to that of the other, like the cold Fit of an Ague to the hot, without any good temper between.

The flatness of their Land exposes it to the danger of the Sea, and forces them to infinite Charge, in the continual Fences and Repairs of their Banks to oppose it; Which employ yearly more Men, than all the Corn of the Province of *Holland* could maintain, (as one of their chief Ministers has told me.) They have lately found the common Seaweed to be the best Material for these Digues, which fastens with a thin mixture of Earth, yields a little to the force of the Sea, and returns when the Waves give back: Whether, they are thereby the safer against Water, as, they say, Houses that shake are against Wind; or whether, as pious Naturalists observe, all things carry about them that which serves for a Remedy against the mischiefs they do in the World.

The extreme moisture of the Air, I take to be the occasion of the great neatness in their Houses, and cleanliness in their Towns. For without the help of those Customs, their Country would not be habitable by such crowds of People, but the Air would corrupt upon every hot season, and expose the Inhabitants to general and infectious Diseases; Which they hardly escape three Summers together, especially about *Leyden*, where the Waters are not so easily renewed, and for this reason, I suppose, it is, that *Leyden* is found to be the neatest and cleanliest kept, of all their Towns.

The same moisture of Air makes all Metals apt to rust, and Wood to mould; which forces them, by continual pains of rubbing and scouring, to seek a Prevention, or Cure: This makes the brightness and cleanness that seems affected in their Houses, and is call'd natural to them, by people who think no further. So the deepness of their Soil, and wetness of Seasons, which would render it unpassable, forces them, not only to exactness of Paving in their Streets, but to the expence of so long Cawsies between many of their Towns, and in their High-ways. As indeed, most National Customs are the Effect of some unseen, or unobserved, natural Causes, or Necessities.

CHAPTER IV

Of their People and Dispositions

The People of *Holland* may be divided into these several Classes: The Clowns or Boors, (as they call them,) who cultivate the Land. The Mariners or Schippers, who supply their Ships, and Inland-Boats. The Merchants, or Traders, who fill their Towns. The *Renteeners*, or Men that live in all their chief Cities upon the Rents or Interest of Estates formerly acquired in their Families: And the Gentlemen, and Officers of their Armies.

The first are a race of People diligent rather than laborious; dull and slow of Understanding, and so not dealt with by hasty words, but managed easily by soft and fair; and yielding to plain Reason, if you give them time to understand it. In the Country and Villages, not too near the great Towns, they seem plain and honest, and content with their own; so that if, in bounty, you give them a Shilling for what is worth but a Groat, they will take the current price, and give you the rest again; if you bid them take it, they know not what you mean, and sometimes ask, if you are a Fool. They know no other Good, but the supply of what Nature requires, and the common increase of Wealth. They feed most upon Herbs, Roots, and Milks; and by that means, I suppose, neither their Strength, nor Vigor, seems answerable to the Size, or Bulk, of their Bodies.

The Mariners are a plain, but much rougher, People; whether from the Element they live in, or from their Food, which is generally Fish, and Corn, and heartier than that of the Boors. They are Surly, and Ill-manner'd, which is

mistaken for Pride; but, I believe, is learnt, as all Manners
are, by the conversation we use. Now theirs lying only
among one another, or with Winds and Waves, which are
not mov'd or wrought upon by any Language, or Observance; or to be dealt with, but by Pains, and by Patience;
These are all the Qualities their Mariners have learnt; their
Valour is *Passive* rather than *Active*; and their Language is
little more, than what is of necessary use to their Business.

The Merchants and Trades-men, both the greater and
Mechanick, living in Towns that are of great resort, both
by Strangers and Passengers of their own, are more
Mercurial, (Wit being sharpned by Commerce and Conversation of Cities,) though they are not very inventive,
which is the gift of warmer Heads; yet are they great in
imitation, and so far, many times, as goes beyond the
Originals: Of mighty Industry, and constant Application
to the Ends they propose and persue. They make use of
their Skill, and their Wit, to take advantage of other Mens
Ignorance and Folly, they deal with: Are great Exacters,
where the Law is in their own Hands. In other Points,
where they deal with Men that understand like themselves,
and are under the reach of Justice and Laws, they are the
plainest and best dealers in the World; Which seems not to
grow so much from a Principle of Conscience, or Morality,
as from a Custom or Habit introduced by the necessity of
Trade among them, which depends as much upon Common-
Honesty, as War does upon Discipline; and without which,
all would break up, Merchants would turn Pedlars, and
Soldiers Thieves.

Those Families which live upon their Patrimonial
Estates in all the great Cities, are a People differently bred
and manner'd from the Traders, though like them in the

modesty of Garb and Habit, and the Parsimony of living. Their Youth are generally bred up at Schools, and at the Universities of *Leyden* or *Utretcht*, in the common studies of Human Learning, but chiefly of the Civil Law, which is that of their Country, at least as far as it is so in *France* and *Spain*. (For, as much as I understand of those Countrys, no Decisions or Decrees of the Civil Law, nor Constitutions of the *Roman* Emperors, have the force or current of Law among them, as is commonly believed, but only the force of Reasons when alledged before their Courts of Judicature, as far as the Authority of Men esteemed wise, passes for Reason: But the ancient Customs of those several Countrys, and the Ordonnances of their Kings and Princes, consented to by the Estates, or in *France* verified by Parliaments, have only the strength and Authority of Law among them.)

Where these Families are rich, their Youths, after the course of their studies at home, travel for some years, as the Sons of our Gentry use to do; but their Journeys are chiefly into *England* and *France*, not much into *Italy*, seldomer into *Spain*, nor often into the more Northern Countrys, unless in company or train of their publick Ministers. The chief end of their Breeding, is, to make them fit for the service of their Country in the Magistracy of their Towns, their Provinces, and their State. And of these kind of Men are the Civil Officers of this Government generally composed, being descended of Families, who have many times been constantly in the Magistracy of their Native Towns for many Years, and some for several Ages.

Such were most or all of the chief Ministers, and the persons that composed their chief Councils, in the time of my residence among them, and not Men of mean or

Mechanick Trades, as it is commonly received among Foreigners, and makes the subject of Comical Jests upon their Government. This does not exclude many Merchants, or Traders in gross, from being often seen in the Offices of their Cities, and sometimes deputed to their States; Nor several of their States, from turning their Stocks in the management of some very beneficial Trade by Servants, and Houses maintained to that purpose. But the generality of the States and Magistrates are of the other sort; Their Estates consisting in the Pensions of their Publick Charges, in the Rents of Lands, or Interest of Money upon the *Cantores*, or in Actions of the *East-Indy* Company, or in Shares upon the Adventures of great Trading-Merchants.

Nor do these Families, habituated as it were to the Magistracy of their Towns and Provinces, usually arrive at great or excessive Riches; The Salaries of Publick Employments and Interest being low, but the Revenue of Lands being yet very much lower, and seldom exceeding the profit of Two in the Hundred. They content themselves with the honour of being useful to the Publick, with the esteem of their Cities or their Country, and with the ease of their Fortunes; which seldom fails, by the frugality of their living, grown universal by being (I suppose) at first necessary, but since honourable, among them.

The mighty growth and excess of Riches is seen among the Merchants and Traders, whose application lyes wholly that way, and who are the better content to have so little share in the Government, desiring only security in what they possess; Troubled with no cares but those of their Fortunes, and the management of their Trades, and turning the rest of their time and thought to the divertisement of their lives. Yet these, when they attain great wealth, chuse to breed up their Sons in the way, and Marry their Daughters into the Families of those others most generally credited in their Towns, and versed in their Magistracies; And thereby introduce their Families into the way of Government and Honour, which consists not here in Titles, but in Publick Employments.

The next Rank among them, is that of their Gentlemen or Nobles, who, in the Province of *Holland*, (to which I chiefly confine these Observations,) are very few, most of the Families having been extinguished in the long Wars with *Spain*. But those that remain, are in a manner all employ'd in the Military or Civil Charges of the Province or State. These are, in their Customs, and Manners, and way of living, a good deal different from the rest of the People; and having been bred much abroad, rather affect the Garb of their Neighbour-Courts, than the Popular Air of their own Country. They value themselves more upon their Nobility, than Men do in other Countrys, where 'tis more common; and would think themselves utterly dishonoured by the Marriage of one that were not of their Rank, though it were to make up the broken Fortune of a Noble Family, by the Wealth of a *Plebean*. They strive to imitate the *French* in their Meen, their Cloathes, their way of Talk, of Eating, of Gallantry or Debauchery; And are, in my mind, something worse than they would be, by affecting to be better than they need; making sometimes but ill Copies, whereas they might be good Originals, by refining or improving the Customs and Virtues proper to their own Country and Climate. They are otherwise an Honest, Well-natur'd, Friendly, and Gentlemanly sort of Men, and acquit themselves generally with Honour and Merit, where their Country employs them.

The Officers of their Armies live after the Customs and Fashions of the Gentlemen; And so do many Sons of the rich Merchants, who, returning from travel abroad, have more designs upon their own pleasure, and the vanity of appearing, than upon the Service of their Country; Or, if they pretend to enter into that, it is rather by the Army than the State. And all these are generally desirous to see a Court in their Country, that they may value themselves at home, by the Qualities they have learnt abroad; and make a Figure, which agrees better with their own Humour, and the manner of Courts, than with the Customs and Orders, that prevail in more Popular Governments.

There are some Customs, or Dispositions, that seem to run generally through all these Degrees of Men among them; As great Frugality, and order, in their Expences. Their common Riches lye in every Man's having more than he spends; or, to say it more properly, In every man's spending less than he has coming in, be that what it will: Nor does it enter into Men's heads among them, That the common port or course of Expence should equal the Revenue; and when this happens, they think at least they have liv'd that year to no purpose; And the train of it discredits a Man among them, as much as any vitious or prodigal Extravagance does in other Countrys. This enables every Man to bear their extream Taxes, and makes them less sensible than they would be in other places: For he that lives upon Two parts in Five of what he has coming in, if he pays Two more to the State, he does but part with what he should have laid up, and had no present use for; Whereas, he that spends yearly what he receives, if he pays but the Fiftieth part to the Publick, it goes from him like that which was necessary to buy Bread or Clothes for himself or his Family.

This makes the beauty and strength of their Towns, the commodiousness of travelling in their Country by their Canals, Bridges, and Cawseys; the pleasantness of their Walks, and their Grafts in and near all their Cities; And in short, the Beauty, Convenience, and sometimes Magnificence, of their Publique Works, to which every Man pays as willingly, and takes as much pleasure and vanity in them, as those of other Countrys do in the same circumstances, among the Possessions of their Families, or private Inheritance. What they can spare, besides the necessary expence of their Domestick, the Publick Payments, and the common course of still encreasing their Stock, is laid out in the Fabrick, Adornment, or Furniture of their Houses: Things not so transitory, or so prejudicial to Health, and to Business, as the constant Excesses and Luxury of Tables; Nor perhaps altogether so vain as the extravagant Expences of Clothes and Attendance; At least, these end wholly in a Man's self, and the satisfaction of his personal Humour; whereas the other make not only the Riches of a Family, but contribute much towards the publick Beauty and Honour of a Country.

The order in casting up their Expences is so great and general, that no Man offers at any Undertaking, which he is not prepared for, and Master of his Design, before he begins; so as I have neither observed nor heard of any Building publick or private, that has not been finished in the time designed for it. So are their Canals, Cawseys, and Bridges; so was their way from the *Hague* to *Skeveling*, a Work that might have become the old *Romans*, considering how soon it was dispatcht. The House at the *Hague*, built purposely for casting of Cannon, was finisht in one Summer, during the heat of the first *English* War, and lookt rather like a design of Vanity in their Government, than Necessity or Use. The Stadthouse of *Amsterdam* has been left purposely to time, without any limitation in the first Design, either of that, or of Expence; both that the Diligence and the Genius of so many succeeding Magistrates should be employ'd in the collection of all things, that could be esteemed proper to encrease the Beauty or Magnificence of that Structure; And perhaps a little to reprieve the experiment of a current Prediction, That the Trade of that City should begin to fall the same year the Stadthouse should be finisht, as it did at *Antwerp*.

Charity seems to be very National among them, though it be regulated by Orders of the Country, and not usually mov'd by the common Objects of Compassion. But it is seen in the admirable Provisions that are made out of it for all sorts of Persons that can want, or ought to be kept, in a Government. Among the many and various Hospitals, that are in every Man's curiosity and talk that travels their Country, I was affected with none more than that of the aged Sea-Men at *Enchusyen*, which is contrived, finished, and ordered, as if it were done with a kind intention of some well-natur'd Man, That those, who had past their whole lives in the Hardships and Incommodities of the Sea, should find a Retreat stor'd with all the Eases and Conveniences, that Old-age is capable of feeling and enjoying. And here I met with the only rich Man, that I ever saw in my life: For one of these old Sea-Men entertaining me a good while with the plain Stories of his Fifty years Voyages and Adventures, while I was viewing their Hospital, and the Church adjoining; I gave him at parting a piece of their Coin about the value of a Crown; He took it smiling, and offer'd it me again; but when I refused it, he askt me, what he should do

with Money? for all that ever they wanted, was provided for
them at their House. I left him to overcome his Modesty as
he could; but a Servant coming after me, saw him give it to
a little Girl that open'd the Church door, as she past by him;
Which made me reflect upon the fantastick calculation of
Riches and Poverty that is current in the World, by which
a Man that wants a Million, is a Prince; He that wants but a
Groat, is a Beggar; and this was a poor Man, that wanted
nothing at all.

In general, All Appetites and Passions seem to run lower
and cooler here, than in other Countrys where I have
converst. Avarice may be excepted. And yet that should
not be so violent, where it feeds only upon Industry and
Parsimony, as where it breaks out into Fraud, Rapine, and
Oppression. But Quarrels are seldom seen among them,
unless in their Drink, Revenge rarely heard of, or Jealousie
known. Their Tempers are not aiery enough for Joy, or any
unusual strains of pleasant Humour; nor warm enough for
Love. This is talkt of sometimes among the younger Men,
but as a thing they have heard of, rather than felt; and as a
discourse that becomes them, rather than affects them. I
have known some among them, that personated Lovers
well enough; but none that I ever thought were at heart in
Love; Nor any of the Women, that seem'd at all to care
whether they were so or no. Whether it be, that they are
such lovers of their Liberty, as not to bear the servitude of a
Mistress, any more than that of a Master; Or, that the
dulness of their Air render them less susceptible of more
refined Passions; Or, that they are diverted from it by the
general intention every Man has upon his business, whatever it is; (nothing being so mortal an Enemy of Love, that
suffers no Rival, as any bent of thought another way.)

The same Causes may have had the same Effects among their Married Women, who have the whole care and absolute management of all their Domestick; And live with very general good Fame; A certain sort of Chastity being hereditary and habitual among them, as Probity among the Men.

The same dulness of Air may dispose them to that strange assiduity and constant application of their Minds, with that perpetual Study and Labour upon any thing they design and take in hand. This gives them patience to persue the quest of Riches by so long Voyages and Adventures to the *Indies*, and by so long Parsimony as that of their whole Lives. Nay, I have (for a more particular example of this Disposition among them,) known one Man that was employ'd Four and Twenty years about the making and perfecting of a Globe, and another above Thirty about the inlaying of a Table. Nor does any Man know, how much may have been contributed towards the great things in all kinds, both publick and private, that have been atchieved among them by this one Humour of never giving over what they imagine may be brought to pass, nor leaving one scent to follow another they meet with; Which is the property of the lighter and more ingenious Nations; And the Humour of a Government being usually the same with that of the persons that compose it, not only in this, but in all other points; so as, where Men that govern, are Wise, Good, Steddy and Just, the Government will appear so too; and the contrary, where they are otherwise.

The same Qualities in their Air may encline them to the Entertainments and Customs of Drinking, which are so much laid to their charge, and, for ought I know, may not only be necessary to their Health, (as they generally believe it,) but to the vigour and improvement of their Understandings, in the midst of a thick foggy Air, and so much coldness of Temper and Complexion. For though the use or excess of Drinking may destroy Men's Abilities who live in better Climates, and are of warmer Constitutions; Wine to hot Brains being like Oyl to Fire, and making the Spirits, by too much lightness, evaporate into smoak, and perfect aiery imaginations; Or, by too much heat, rage into Frenzy, or at least into Humours and Thoughts, that have a great mixture of it; Yet on the other side, it may improve Men's Parts and Abilities of cold Complexions, and in dull Air; and may be necessary to thaw and move the frozen or unactive Spirits of the Brain; To rowse sleepy Thought, and refine grosser Imaginations, and perhaps to animate the Spirits of the Heart, as well as enliven those of the Brain: Therefore the old *Germans* seem'd to have some reason in their Custom, not to execute any great Resolutions which had not been twice debated, and agreed at two several Assemblies, one in an Afternoon, and t'other in a Morning; Because, they thought, their Counsels might want Vigour when they were sober, as well as Caution when they had drunk.

Yet in *Holland* I have observed very few of their chief Officers or Ministers of State vitious in this kind; Or, if they drunk much, 'twas only at set Feasts, and rather to acquit themselves, than of choice or inclination; And for the Merchants and Traders, with whom it is customary, They never do it in a Morning, nor till they come from the Exchange, where the business of the day is commonly dispatcht; Nay, it hardly enters into their Heads, that 'tis lawful to drink at all before that time; but they will excuse it, if you come to their House, and tell you how sorry they are you come in a Morning, when they cannot offer you to drink; as if at that time of day it were not only unlawful for them to drink themselves, but so much as for a stranger to do it within their Walls.

The Afternoon, or, at least, the Evening is given to whatever they find will divert them; And is no more than needs, considering how they spend the rest of the day, in Thought, or in Cares; in Toils, or in Business. For Nature cannot hold out with constant labour of Body, and as little with constant bent, or application, of Mind: Much motion of the same parts of the Brain either wearies and wasts them too fast for repair, or else (as it were) fires the wheels, and so ends, either in general decays of the Body, or distractions of the Mind (For these are usually occasion'd by perpetual motions of Thought about some one Object; whether it be about ones self in excesses of Pride, or about another in those of Love, or of Grief.) Therefore none are so excusable as Men of much Care and Thought, or of great business, for giving up their times of leisure to any pleasures or diversions that offend no Laws, nor hurt others or themselves: And this seems the reason, that, in all Civil Constitutions, not only Honours, but Riches, are annexed to the Charges of those who govern, and upon whom the Publique Cares are meant to be devolved; Not only, that they may not be distracted from these, by the Cares of their own Domestique or private Interests; but, that by the help of Esteem, and of Riches, they may have those Pleasures and Diversions in their reach, which idle Men neither need nor deserve, but which are necessary for the refreshment, or repair, of Spirits, exhausted with Cares, and with Toil, and which serve to sweeten and preserve those Lives that would otherwise wear out too fast, or grow too uneasie in the Service of the Publique.

The Two Characters, that are left by the old *Roman* Writers, of the ancient *Batavi* or *Hollanders*, are, That they were both the bravest among the *German* Nations, and the most obstinate Lovers and Defenders of their Liberty[1]; Which made them exempted from all Tribute by the *Romans*, who desir'd only Soldiers of their Nation, to make up some of their Auxiliary-Bands, as they did in former Ages of those Nations in *Italy* that were their Friends, and Allies[2]. The last disposition seems to have continued constant and National among them, ever since that time, and never to have more appeared, than in the Rise and Constitutions of their present State. It does not seem to be so of the First, or that the People in general can be said now to be Valiant, a quality, of old, so National among them, and which, by the several Wars of the Counts of *Holland*, (especially with the *Frizons*,) and by the desperate Defences made against the *Spaniards*, by this People, in the beginnings of their State, should seem to have lasted long, and to have but lately decayed; That is, since the whole application of their Natives has been turn'd to Commerce and Trade, and the vein of their Domestique Lives so much to Parsimony, (by Circumstances which will be the subject of another Chapter;) and since the main of all their Forces, and body of their Army, has been composed, and continually supplied out of their Neighbour-Nations.

For Soldiers and Merchants are not found, by experience, to be more incompatible in their abode, than the Dispositions and Customs seem to be different, that render a

[1] Queruntur (Fabii Valentis) Legiones, orbari se fortissimorum virorum auxilio, veteres illos & tot bellorum auctores non abrumpendos ut corpori validissimos artus. *Tacit. Hist.*

[2] Omnium harum gentium virtute praecipui Batavi non multum ex ripâ sed Insulam Rheni amnis colunt. *Tacit. de Mor. Ger.*

People fit for Trade, and for War. The Soldier thinks of a short life and a merry. The Trader thinks upon a long, and a painful. One intends to make his Fortunes suddenly by his Courage, by Victory, and Spoil: The t'other slower, but surer, by Craft, by Treaty, and by Industry. This makes the first franc and generous, and throw away, upon his Pleasures, what has been gotten in one Danger, and may either be lost, or repaired, in the next. The other wary and frugal, and loath to part with in a day, what he has been labouring for a Year, and has no hopes to recover, but by the same paces of Diligence and Time. One aims only to preserve what he has, as the fruit of his Father's pains; or what he shall get, as the fruit of his own: T'other thinks the price of a little Blood is more than of a great deal of Sweat; and means to live upon other Men's Labours, and possess in an hour, what they have been years in acquiring: This makes one love to live under stanch Orders and Laws; While t'other would have all depend upon Arbitrary Power and Will. The Trader reckons upon growing Richer, and by his account Better, the longer he lives; which makes him careful of his Health, and his Life, and so apt to be orderly and temperate in his Diet; While the Soldier is Thoughtless, or prodigal of both; and having not his Meat ready at hours, or when he has a mind to it, Eats full and greedily, whenever he gets it; And perhaps difference of Diet may make greater difference in men's natural Courage, than is commonly Thought of.

For Courage may proceed, in some measure, from the temper of Air, may be form'd by Discipline, and acquir'd by Use, or infus'd by Opinion; But that which is more natural, and so more National in some Countries than in others, seems to arise from the heat or strength of Spirits about the Heart, which may a great deal depend upon the measure and the substance of the Food, Men are used to. This made a great Physician among us say, He would make any Man a Coward with six weeks Dieting; and Prince *Maurice* of *Orange* call for the *English* that were newly come over, and had (as he said) their own Beef in their Bellies, for any bold and desperate Action. This may be one reason, why the Gentry, in all places of the World, are braver than the Peasantry, whose Hearts are depressed, not only by Slavery, but by short and heartless Food, the effect of their Poverty. This is a cause, why the Yeomanry and Commonalty of *England* are generally braver than in other Countries, because by the Plenty, and Constitutions, of the Kingdom, they are so much easier in their Rents and their Taxes, and fare so much better and fuller, than those, of their rank, in any other Nation. Their chief, and, indeed, constant food, being of Flesh; And among all Creatures, both the Birds and the Beasts, we shall still find those that feed upon Flesh, to be the fierce and the bold; and on the contrary, the fearful and faint-hearted to feed upon Grass, and upon Plants. I think, there can be pretended but two Exceptions to this Rule, which are the Cock and the Horse; whereas the Courage of the One, is noted no where but in *England*, and there, only in certain Races: And for the Other, all the Courage we commend in them, is, the want of Fear; and they are observed to grow much fiercer, when-ever by custom, or necessity, they have been used to flesh.

From all this may be inferr'd, That not only the long disuse of Arms among the Native *Hollanders*, (especially at Land,) and making use of other Nations, chiefly in their Milice; But the Arts of Trade, as well as Peace, and their great Parsimony in Diet, and eating so very little Flesh, (which the common People seldom do, above once a week,) may have helpt to debase much the ancient valour of the Nation, at least, in the occasions of Service at Land. Their Seamen are much better; but not so good as those of *Zealand*, who are generally brave; Which, I suppose, comes by these having upon all occasions turn'd so much more to Privateering, and Men of War; and those of *Holland*, being generally employ'd in Trading and Merchant-Ships; While their Men of War are Mann'd by Mariners of all Nations, who are very numerous among them, but especially, those of the *Eastland* Coasts of *Germany*, *Suedes*, *Danes*, and *Norwegians*.

'Tis odd, that Veins of Courage should seem to run like Veins of good Earth in a Country, and yet not only those of the Province of *Hainault* among the *Spanish*, and of *Gelderland* among the *United Provinces*, are esteemed better Soldiers than the rest; But the Burghers of *Valenciennes* among the Towns of *Flanders*, and of *Nimmeguen* among those of the lower *Gelder*, are observed to be particularly brave. But there may be firmness and constancy of Courage from Tradition, as well as of Belief: Nor methinks should any Man know how to be a Coward, that is brought up with the Opinion, That all his Nation or City have ever been valiant.

I can say nothing of what is usually laid to their charge, about their being Cruel, besides, what we have so often heard of their barbarous usage to some of our Men in the *East-Indies*, and what we have so lately seen of their Savage Murther of their *Pensioner de Wit*; A Person that deserv'd another Fate, and a better return from his Country, after Eighteen years spent in their Ministry, without any care of his Entertainments or Ease, and little of his Fortune.

A Man of unwearied Industry, inflexible Constancy, sound, clear, and deep Understanding, with untainted Integrity; so that whenever he was blinded, it was by the passion he had for that which he esteemed the good and interest of his State. This testimony is justly due to him from all that practised him; and is the more willingly paid, since there can be as little interest to flatter, as honour to reproach, the dead. But this action of that people may be attributed to the misfortune of their Country; and is so unlike the appearance of their Customs and Dispositions, living, as I saw them, under the Orders and Laws of a quiet and setled State, and one must confess Mankind to be a very various Creature, and none to be known, that has not been seen in his Rage, as well as his Drink.

They are generally not so long liv'd, as in better Airs; and begin to decay early, both Men and Women, especially at *Amsterdam*; For, at the *Hague*, (which is their best Air) I have known two considerable Men, a good deal above Seventy, and one of them in very good Sense and Health: But this is not so usual as it is in *England*, and in *Spain*. The Diseases of the Climate seem to be chiefly the Gout and the Scurvy; but all hot and dry Summers bring some that are infectious among them, especially into *Amsterdam* and *Leyden*: These are usually Fevers, that lye most in the Head, and either kill suddenly, or languish long before they recover. Plagues are not so frequent, at least not in a degree to be taken notice of, for All suppress the talk of them as much as they can, and no distinction is made in the Registry of the dead, nor much in the Care and Attendance of the Sick: Whether from a belief of Predestination, or else, a Preference of Trade, which is the life of the Country, before that of particular Men.

Strangers among them are apt to complain·of the Spleen, but those of the Country seldom or never: Which I take to proceed from their being ever busie, or easily satisfied. For this seems to be the Disease of People that are idle, or think themselves but ill entertain'd, and attribute every fit of dull Humour, or Imagination, to a formal Disease, which they have found this Name for; Whereas, such Fits are incident to all Men, at one time or other, from the fumes of In-digestion, from the common alterations of some insensible degrees in Health and vigor[1]; or, from some changes or approaches of change in Winds and Weather, which affect the finer Spirits of the Brain, before they grow sensible to other parts; And are apt to alter the shapes, or colours, of whatever is represented to us by our Imaginations, whilst we are so affected. Yet this Effect is not so strong, but that business, or intention of Thought, commonly either resists, or diverts, it; And those who understand the motions of it, let it pass, and return to themselves. But such as are idle, or know not from whence these changes arise, and trouble their Heads with Notions, or Schemes of general Happiness, or Unhappiness, in life, upon every such Fit, begin Reflections on the condition of their Bodies, their Souls, or their Fortunes; And (as all things are then repre-sented in the worst colours) they fall into melancholy apprehensions of one or other, and sometimes of them all: These make deep impression in their Minds, and are not

[1]   Ubi tempestas & coeli mobilis humor
       Mutavere vias, & Jupiter humidus Austris,
       Densat, erant quae rara modo, & quae densa relaxat
       Vertuntur species animorum, & pectora motus
       Nunc alios, alios dum nubila ventus agebat
       Concipiunt, hinc ille avium concentus in agris
       Et laetae pecudes, & ovantes gutture corvi.
                    Virg. Georg.

easily worn out by the natural returns of good Humour, especially if they are often interrupted by the contrary; As happens in some particular Constitutions, and more generally in uncertain Climates, especially, if improved by accidents of ill Health, or ill Fortune. But this is a Disease too refin'd for this Country and People, who are well, when they are not ill; and pleas'd, when they are not troubled; are content, because they think little of it: and seek their Happiness in the common Eases and Commodities of Life, or the encrease of Riches; Not amusing themselves with the more speculative contrivances of Passion, or refinements of Pleasure.

To conclude this Chapter: *Holland* is a Country, where the Earth is better than the Air, and Profit more in request than Honour; Where there is more Sense than Wit; More good Nature than good Humor; And more Wealth than Pleasure; Where a Man would chuse rather to Travel, than to Live; Shall find more things to observe than desire; And more Persons to esteem than to love. But the same Qualities and Dispositions do not value a private Man and a State, nor make a Conversation agreeable, and a Government Great: Nor is it unlikely, that some very great King might make but a very ordinary private Gentleman, and some very extraordinary Gentleman, might be capable of making but a very mean Prince.

CHAPTER V

Of their Religion

I Intend not here to speak of Religion at all as a Divine, but as a mere Secular Man, when I observe the occasions that seem to have establisht it in the Forms, or with the Liberties, wherewith it is now attended in the *United Provinces*. I believe, the Reformed Religion was introduced there, as well as in *England*, and the many other Countries where it is profess'd, by the operation of Divine Will and Providence; And by the same, I believe the *Roman Catholique* was continued in *France*: Where it seemed, by the conspiring of so many Accidents in the beginning of *Charles* the Ninth's Reign, to be so near a change. And whoever doubts this, seems to question not only the Will, but the Power, of God. Nor will it at all derogate from the Honour of a Religion, to have been planted in a Country, by Secular means, or Civil Revolutions, which have, long since, succeeded to those Miraculous Operations that made way for Christianity in the World. 'Tis enough, that God Almighty infuses belief into the Hearts of Men, or else, ordains it to grow out of Religious Enquiries and Instructions; And that wherever the generality of a Nation come by these means to be of a belief, it is by the force of this concurrence introduced into the Government, and becomes the establisht Religion of That Country. So was the Reformed Profession introduced into *England, Scotland, Sueden, Denmark, Holland,* and many parts of *Germany.* So was the *Roman-Catholique* restored in *France* and in *Flanders*; where, notwithstanding the great Concussions that were made in the Government by the *Hugonots* and the *Gueuses*, yet they were never esteemed, in either of those Countries, to amount further than the Seventh or Eighth part of the People. And whosoever designs the change of Religion in a Country, or Government, by any other means than that of a general conversion of the People, or the greatest part of them, designs all the Mischiefs to a Nation, that use to usher in, or attend, the two greatest Distempers of a State, Civil War, or Tyranny; Which are Violence, Oppression, Cruelty, Rapine, Intemperance, Injustice, and, in short, the miserable Effusion of Human Blood, and the Confusion of all Laws, Orders, and Virtues, among Men.

Such Consequences as these, I doubt, are something more than the disputed Opinions of any Man, or any particular Assembly of Men, can be worth; since the great and general End of all Religion, next to Men's Happiness hereafter, is their Happiness here; As appears by the Commandments of God, being the best and greatest Moral and Civil, as well as Divine, Precepts, that have been given to a Nation; And by the Rewards proposed to the Piety of the *Jews*, throughout the Old Testament, which were the Blessings of this Life, as Health, length of Age, number of Children, Plenty, Peace, or Victory.

Now the way to our future Happiness, has been perpetually disputed throughout the World, and must be left, at last, to the Impressions made upon every Man's Belief, and Conscience, either by natural, or supernatural, Arguments and Means; which Impressions Men may disguise or dissemble, but no Man can resist. For Belief is no more in a Man's Power, than his Stature, or his Feature; And he that tells me, I must change my Opinion for his, because 'tis the truer and the better, without other Arguments, that

have to me the force of Conviction, may as well tell me, I
must change my Grey Eyes, for others like his that are
Black, because these are lovelier, or more in esteem. He
that tells me, I must inform my Self; Has reason, if I do it
not: But if I endeavour it all that I can, and perhaps, more
than he ever did, and yet still differ from him; And he, that,
it may be, is idle, will have me study on, and inform myself
better, and so to the end of my life; Then I easily understand what he means by informing, which is, in short, that
I must do it, till I come to be of his Opinion.

If he, that, perhaps, persues his Pleasures or Interests, as
much, or more, than I do; And allows me to have as good
Sense, as he has in all other matters, tells me I should be of
his opinion, but that Passion or Interest blinds me; unless
he can convince me how, or where, this lies, he is but where
he was, only pretends to know me better than I do my self,
who cannot imagine, why I should not have as much care of
my Soul, as he has of His.

A man that tells me, my Opinions are absurd or ridi-
culous, impertinent or unreasonable, because they differ
from His, seems to intend a Quarrel instead of a Dispute;
and calls me Fool, or Mad-man, with a little more circumstance; though, perhaps, I pass for one as well in my senses
as he, as pertinent in talk, and as prudent in life: Yet these
are the common Civilities, in Religious Argument, of
sufficient and conceited men, who talk much of Right
Reason, and mean always their own; and make their
private imagination the measure of general Truth. But
such language determines all between us, and the Dispute
comes to end in three words at last, which it might as well
have ended in at first, That he is in the right, and I am in the
wrong.

The other great End of Religion, which is our Happiness here, has been generally agreed on by all Mankind, as appears in the Records of all their Laws, as well as all their Religions, which come to be establisht by the concurrence of Men's Customs and Opinions[1]; though in the latter, that concurrence may have been produced by Divine Impressions or Inspirations. For all agree in Teaching and Commanding, in Planting and Improving, not only those Moral Virtues, which conduce to the felicity and tranquillity of every private Man's Life; but also those Manners and Dispositions that tend to the Peace, Order, and Safety of all Civil Societies and Governments among Men. Nor could I ever understand, how those, who call themselves, and the World usually calls, *Religious Men*, come to put so great weight upon those Points of Belief which Men never have agreed in, and so little upon those of Virtue and Morality, in which they have hardly ever disagreed. Nor, why a State should venture the Subversion of their Peace, and their Order, which are certain Goods, and so universally esteemed, for the propagation of uncertain or contested Opinions.

One of the great Causes of the first Revolt in the *Low-Countries*, appeared to be, The Oppression of Mens Consciences, or Persecution in their Liberties, their Estates and their Lives, upon pretence of Religion. And this at a time, when there seemed to be a conspiring Disposition in most Countries of Christendom, to seek the Reformation of some abuses, grown in the Doctrine and Discipline of the Church, either by the Rust of time, by Negligence, or by Human Inventions, Passions and

[1] Fiunt diversae respublicae ex civium moribus, qui, quocunq; fluxerint caetera secum rapiunt. *Plat. de Rep.*

Interests. The rigid opposition given at *Rome* to this general Humour, was followed by a defection of mighty numbers in all those several Countries, who professed to reform themselves, acording to such Rules as they thought were necessary for the Reformation of the Church. These persons, though they agreed in the main of disowning the Papal Power, and reducing Belief from the Authority of Tradition to That of the Scripture; Yet they differ'd much among themselves in other circumstances, especially of Discipline, according to the Persuasions and Impressions of the Leading Doctors in their several Countrys. So the Reformed of *France* became universally *Calvinists*; But for those of *Germany*, though they were generally *Lutherans*, yet there was a great mixture both of *Calvinists* and *Anabaptists* among them.

The first Persecutions of these Reformed arose in *Germany*, in the time of *Charles* the Fifth, and drove great numbers of them down into the Seventeen Provinces, especially *Holland* and *Brabant*, where the Priviledges of the Cities were greater, and the Emperor's Government was less severe, as among the Subjects of his own Native Countrys. This was the occasion, that in the year 1566. when, upon the first Insurrection in *Flanders*, those of the Reformed Profession began to form Consistories, and levy Contributions among themselves, for support of their Common Cause; It was resolved, upon consultation, among the Heads of them, that for declining all differences among themselves, at a time of common exigence, The publick Profession of their Party should be That of the *Lutherans*, though with liberty and indulgence to those of different Opinions. By the Union of *Utrecht* concluded in 1579, Each of the Provinces was left to order the matter of

Religion, as they thought fit and most conducing to the
welfare of their Province; With this provision, that every
man should remain free in his Religion, and none be
examined or entrapped for that cause, according to the
Pacification at *Gant*. But in the year 1583, it was enacted by
general agreement, That the Evangelical Religion should
be only professed in all the Seven Provinces: Which came
thereby to be the establisht Religion of this State.

The Reasons, which seemed to induce them to this
settlement, were many, and of weight; As first, because by
the Persecutions arrived in *France*, (where all the Reformed
were *Calvinists*) multitudes of People had retired out of that
Kingdom into the *Low-Countrys*; And by the great commerce and continual intercourse with *England*, where the
Reformation agreed much with the *Calvinists* in point of
Doctrine, though more with the *Lutherans* in point of
Discipline, Those Opinions came to be credited and pro-
pagated more than any other, among the people of these
Provinces, so as the numbers were grown to be greater far
in the Cities of This than of any other Profession. Secondly,
the Succours and Supplies both of Men and Money, by
which the weak Beginnings of this Commonwealth were
preserved and fortified, came chiefly from *England*, from
the Protestants of *France*, (when their affairs were success-
ful) and from the *Calvinist* Princes of *Germany*, who lay
nearest, and were readiest to relieve them. In the next
place, because those of this Profession seem'd the most
contrary and violent against the *Spaniards*, who made
themselves Heads of the *Roman-Catholicks* throughout
Christendom, and the hatred of *Spain*, and their Dominion
was so rooted in the Hearts of this People, that it had influence upon them in the very choice of their Religion. And

lastly, because, by this Profession, all Rights and Jurisdiction of the Clergy or Hierarchy being suppressed, there was no Ecclesiastical Authority left to rise up and trouble or fetter the Civil Power; And all the Goods and Possessions of Churches and Abbies were seized wholly into the hands of the State, which made a great encrease of the publick Revenue, a thing the most necessary for the support of their Government.

There might perhaps be added one Reason more, which was particular to one of the Provinces: For, whereas in most, if not all, other parts of Christendom, the Clergy composed one of the Three Estates of the Country, and thereby shar'd with the Nobles and Commons in their Influences upon the Government; That Order never made any part of the Estates in *Holland*, nor had any Vote in their Assembly, which consisted only of the Nobles and the Cities; and this Province bearing always the greatest sway in the Councils of the Union, was most enclined to the settlement of that Profession, which gave least pretence of Power or Jurisdiction to the Clergy, and so agreed most with their own ancient Constitutions.

Since this Establishment, as well as before, the great care of this State has ever been, to favour no particular or curious Inquisition into the Faith or Religious Principles of any peaceable Man, who came to live under the protection of their Laws, and to suffer no Violence or Oppression upon any Mans Conscience, whose Opinions broke not out into Expressions or Actions of ill consequence to the State. A free Form of Government either making way for more freedom in Religion; or else, having newly contended so far themselves for Liberty in this point, they thought it the more unreasonable for them to oppress others.   Perhaps

while they were so threatned and endanger'd by Foreign
Armies, they thought it the more necessary to provide
against discontents within, which can never be dangerous,
where they are not grounded or fathered upon Oppression
in point either of Religion or Liberty. But in those two
Cases, the Flame often proves most violent in a State, the
more 'tis shut up, or the longer concealed.

The *Roman Catholick* Religion was alone excepted from
the common protection of their Laws, making Men (as the
States believed) worse Subjects than the rest, by the acknowledgment of a Foreign and Superiour Jurisdiction;
For so must all Spiritual Power needs be, as grounded upon
greater Hopes and Fears than any Civil, at least, where-ever
the persuasions from Faith are as strong as those from
Sense; of which there are so many Testimonies recorded by
the Martyrdoms, Penances, or Conscientious Restraints
and Severities, suffered by infinite Persons in all sorts of
Religions.

Besides, this Profession seemed still a retainer of the
Spanish Government, which was then the great Patron of it
in the world: Yet, such was the care of this State to give all
men ease in this point, who ask no more than to serve God,
and save their own Souls, in their own Way and Forms;
that what was not provided for by the Constitutions of
their Government, was so, in a very great degree, by the
Connivance of their Officers, Who, upon certain constant
Payments from every Family, suffer the exercise of the
Roman-Catholick Religion in their several Jurisdictions, as
free and easie, though not so cheap and so avowed, as the
rest. This, I suppose, has been the reason, that though those
of this Profession are very numerous in the Country,
among the Peasants, and considerable in the Cities; and not

admitted to any publick charges; Yet they seem to be a sound piece of the State, and fast jointed in with the rest; And have neither given any disturbance to the Government, nor exprest any inclinations to a change, or to any Foreign Power, either upon the former Wars with *Spain*, or the later Invasions of the Bishop of *Munster*.

Of all other Religions, every Man enjoys the free exercise in his own Chamber, or his own House, unquestioned and unespied: And if the Followers of any Sect grow so numerous in any place, that they affect a publick Congregation, and are content to purchase a place of Assembly, to bear the charge of a Pastor or Teacher, and to pay for this Liberty to the Publick; They go and propose their desire to the Magistrates of the place where they reside, who inform themselves of their Opinions, and manners of Worship; and if they find nothing in either, destructive to Civil Society, or prejudicial to the Constitutions of their State, and content themselves with the price that is offer'd for the purchase of this Liberty, They easily allow it; But with the condition, That one or more Commissioners shall be appointed, who shall have free admission at all their Meetings, shall be both the Observers and Witnesses of all that is Acted or Preached among them, and whose Testimony shall be received concerning any thing that passes there to the prejudice of the State; In which case, the Laws and Executions are as severe as against any Civil Crimes.

Thus the *Jews* have their allowed Synagogues in *Amsterdam* and *Rotterdam*; And in the first, almost all Sects, that are known among Christians, have their publick Meetingplaces; and some whose Names are almost worn out in all other parts, as the *Brownists*, *Familists*, and others: The *Arminians*, though they make a great Name among them, by being rather the distinction of a Party in the State, than a Sect in the Church; yet are, in comparison of others, but few in number, though considerable by the persons, who are of the better quality, the more learned and intelligent Men, and many of them in the Government. The *Anabaptists* are just the contrary, very numerous, but in the lower ranks of people, Mechanicks and Sea-men, and abound chiefly in *North-Holland.*

The *Calvinists* make the Body of the people, and are possessed of all the publick Churches in the Dominions of the State, as well as of the only Ministers or Pastors, who are maintained by the Publick; But these have neither Lands, nor Tithes, nor any authorized Contributions from the people, but certain Salaries from the State, upon whom they wholly depend: And though they are often very bold in taxing and preaching publickly against the Vices, and somtimes the innocent Entertainments, of persons most considerable in the Government, as well as of the Vulgar; yet they are never heard to censure or controul the publick Actions or Resolutions of the State: They are, in general, throughout the Country, passionate Friends to the Interests of the House of *Orange*; And, during the intermission of that Authority, found ways of expressing their affections to the Person and Fortunes of this Prince, without offending the State, as it was then constituted. They are fierce Enemies of the *Arminian* Party, whose Principles were thought to lead them, in *Barnevelt's* time, towards a conjunction, or at least compliance, with the *Spanish* Religion and Government; Both which, the House of *Orange*, in the whole course of the War, endeavoured to make irreconcileable with those of the State.

It is hardly to be imagined, how all the violence and

sharpness, which accompanies the differences of Religion in other Countrys, seems to be appeased or softned here, by the general freedom which all men enjoy, either by allowance or connivance; Nor, how Faction and Ambition are thereby disabled to colour their Interested and Seditious Designs with the pretences of Religion, which has cost the Christian World so much blood for these last Hundred and fifty years. No man can here complain of pressure in his Conscience; Of being forced to any publick profession of his private Faith; Of being restrained from his own manner of worship in his House, or obliged to any other abroad: And whoever asks more in point of Religion, without the undisputed evidence of a particular Mission from Heaven, may be justly suspected, not to ask for God's sake, but for his own; since pretending to Sovereignty, instead of Liberty, in Opinion, is indeed pretending the same in Authority too, which consists chiefly in Opinion; And what Man, or Party soever, can gain the common and firm belief, of being most immediately inspired, instructed, or favoured of God, will easily obtain the Prerogative of being most honour'd and obey'd by Men.

But in this Commonwealth, no Man having any reason to complain of oppression in Conscience; and no Man having hopes, by advancing his Religion, to form a Party, or break in upon the State, the differences in Opinion make none in Affections, and little in Conversation, where it serves but for entertainment and variety. They argue without interest or anger; They differ without enmity or scorn; and They agree without confederacy. Men live together, like Citizens of the World, associated by the common ties of Humanity, and by the bonds of Peace, under the impartial protection of indifferent Laws, with equal encouragement of all Art and Industry, and equal freedom of

Speculation and Enquiry; All men enjoying their imaginary excellencies and acquisitions of knowledg, with as much safety, as their more real Possessions and Improvements of Fortune. The Power of Religion among them, where it is, lies in every Man's heart; The appearance of it is but like a piece of Humanity, by which every one falls most into the company or conversation of those, whose customs and Humours, whose Talk and Dispositions, he likes best: And as in other places, 'tis in every Man's choice with whom he will eat or lodge, with whom go to Market, or to Court; So it seems to be here, with whom he will Pray or go to Church, or Associate in the Service and Worship of God; Nor is any more notice taken, or more censure past, of what every one chuses in these cases, than in the other.

I believe the force of Commerce, Alliances, and Acquaintance, spreading so far as they do in small Circuits, (such as the Province of *Holland*) may contribute much to make conversation and all the Offices of common life, so easie, among so different Opinions, of which so many several persons are often in every Man's Eye; And no Man checks or takes offence at Faces, or Customs, or Ceremonies, he sees every day, as at those he hears of in places far distant, and perhaps by partial relations, and comes to see late in his life, and after he has long been possest by passion or prejudice against them. However it is, Religion may possibly do more good in other places, but it does less hurt here; And where-ever the invisible effects of it are the greatest and most advantageous, I am sure, the visible are so in this Country, by the continual and undisturbed Civil Peace of their Government for so long a course of years; And by so mighty an encrease of their people, wherein will appear to consist chiefly the vast growth of their Trade and Riches, and consequently the strength and greatness of their State.

CHAPTER VI

Of their Trade

'Tis evident to those, who have read the most, and travel'd farthest, that no Country can be found either in this present Age, or upon Record of any Story, where so vast a Trade has been managed, as in the narrow compass of the Four Maritime Provinces of this Commonwealth: Nay, it is generally esteemed, that they have more Shipping belongs to them, than there does to all the rest of *Europe*. Yet they have no Native Commodities towards the Building or Rigging of the smallest Vessel; Their Flax, Hemp, Pitch, Wood, and Iron, coming all from abroad, as Wool does for cloathing their Men, and Corn for feeding them. Nor do I know any thing properly of their own growth, that is considerable either for their own necessary use, or for Traffick with their Neighbours, besides Butter, Cheese, and Earthen Wares. For Havens, they have not any good upon their whole Coast: The best are *Helversluys*, which has no Trade at all; and *Flussingue*, which has little, in comparison of other Towns in *Holland*: But *Amsterdam*, that triumphs in the spoils of *Lisbon* and *Antwerp*, (which before engrost the greatest Trade of *Europe* and the *Indies*,) seems to be the most incommodious Haven they have, being seated upon so shallow Waters, that ordinary Ships cannot come up to it without the advantage of Tides; Nor great ones without unlading. The entrance of the *Tessel*, and passage over the *Zudder-Sea*, is more dangerous than a Voyage from thence to *Spain*, lying all in blind and narrow Channels; so that it easily appears, that 'tis not an Haven that draws Trade, but Trade that fills an Haven, and brings it in vogue. Nor has *Holland* grown rich by any Native Commodities, but by force of Industry; By improvement and manufacture of all Foreign growths; By being the general Magazine of *Europe*, and furnishing all parts with whatever the Market wants or invites; And by their Sea-men, being, as they have properly been call'd, the common Carriers of the World.

Since the ground of Trade cannot be deduced from Havens, or Native Commodities, (as may well be concluded from the survey of *Holland*, which has the least and the worst; and of *Ireland*, which has the most and the best, of both;) it were not amiss to consider, from what other source it may be more naturally and certainly derived: For if we talk of Industry, we are still as much to seek, what it is that makes people industrious in one Country, and idle in another. I conceive the true original and ground of Trade, to be, great multitude of people crowded into small compass of Land, whereby all things necessary to life become dear, and all Men, who have possessions, are induced to Parsimony; but those who have none, are forced to industry and labour, or else to want. Bodies that are vigorous, fall to labour; Such as are not, supply that defect by some sort of Inventions or Ingenuity. These Customs arise first from Necessity, but encrease by Imitation, and grow in time to be habitual in a Country; And wherever they are so, if it lies upon the Sea, they naturally break out into Trade, both because, whatever they want of their own, that is necessary to so many Mens Lives, must be supply'd from abroad; and because, by the multitude of people, and smalness of Country, Land grows so dear, that the Improvement of Money, that way, is inconsiderable, and so turns to Sea, where the greatness of the Profit makes amends for the Venture.

This cannot be better illustrated, than by its contrary, which appears no where more than in *Ireland*; Where, by the largeness and plenty of the Soil, and scarcity of People, all things necessary to Life are so cheap, that an industrious Man, by two days labour, may gain enough to feed him the rest of the week; Which I take to be a very plain ground of the laziness attributed to the People: For Men naturally prefer Ease before Labour, and will not take pains, if they can live idle; though, when, by necessity, they have been inured to it, they cannot leave it, being grown a custom necessary to their Health, and to their very Entertainment: Nor perhaps is the change harder, from constant Ease to Labour, than from constant Labour to Ease.

This account of the Original of Trade, agrees with the experience of all Ages, and with the Constitutions of all places, where it has most flourished in the World, as *Tyre*, *Carthage*, *Athens*, *Syracuse*, *Agrigentum*, *Rhodes*, *Venice*, *Holland*; and will be so obvious to every Man, that knows and considers the scituation, the extent, and the nature, of all those Countries, that it will need no enlargement upon the comparisons.

By these Examples, which are all of Commonwealths, and, by the decay, or dissolution, of Trade, in the Six first, when they came to be conquered, or subjected to Arbitrary Dominions, it might be concluded, that there is something, in that form of Government, proper and natural to Trade, in a more peculiar manner. But the height it arrived to at *Bruges* and *Antwerp*, under their Princes, for four or five descents of the House of *Burgundy*, and two of *Austria*,

shews, it may thrive under good Princes and Legal Monarchies, as well as under Free States. Under Arbitrary and
Tyrannical Power, it must of necessity decay and dissolve,
because this empties a Country of People, whereas the
others fill it; This extinguishes Industry, whilst Men are in
doubt of enjoying themselves what they get, or leaving it to
their Children; The others encourage it, by securing Men of
both: One fills a Country with Soldiers, and the other with
Merchants; Who were never yet known to live well together, because they cannot trust one another: And as
Trade cannot live without mutual trust among private
Men; so it cannot grow or thrive, to any great degree,
without a confidence both of publick and private safety,
and consequently a trust in the Government, from an
opinion of its Strength, Wisdom, and Justice; Which must
be grounded either upon the Personal Virtues and Qualities
of a Prince, or else upon the Constitutions and Orders of a
State.

It appears to every Mans eye who hath travell'd *Holland*,
and observed the number and vicinity of their great and
populous Towns and Villages, with the prodigious improvement of almost every spot of ground in the Country, and
the great multitudes constantly employ'd in their Shipping
abroad, and their Boats at home, That no other known
Country in the World, of the same extent, holds any
proportion with this in numbers of People; And if that be
the great foundation of Trade, the best account that can be
given of theirs, will be, by considering the Causes and
Accidents, that have served to force or invite so vast a
confluence of People into their Country. In the first rank
may be placed, the Civil-Wars, Calamities, Persecutions,
Oppressions, or Discontents, that have been so fatal to

most of their Neighbours, for some time before as well as since their State began.

The Persecutions for matter of Religion, in *Germany* under *Charles* the Fifth, in *France* under *Henry* the Second, and in *England* under Queen *Mary*, forced great numbers of People out of all those Countrys, to shelter themselves in the several Towns of the Seventeen Provinces, where the ancient Liberties of the Country, and Priviledges of the Cities, had been inviolate under so long a succession of Princes, and gave protection to these oppressed strangers, who fill'd their Cities both with People and Trade, and raised *Antwerp* to such an heigth and renown, as continued till the Duke of *Alva's* arrival in the *Low-Countrys*. The fright of this Man, and the Orders he brought, and Armies to execute them, began to scatter the Flock of People that for some time had been nested there; So as, in very few Months, above a Hundred Thousand Families removed out of the Country. But when the Seven Provinces United, and began to defend themselves with success, under the conduct of the Prince of *Orange*, and the countenance of *England* and *France*, and the Persecutions for Religion began to grow sharp in the *Spanish* Provinces, all the Professors of the Reformed Religion, and haters of the *Spanish* Dominion, retir'd into the strong Cities of this Commonwealth, and gave the same date to the growth of Trade there, and the decay of it at *Antwerp*.

The long Civil-Wars, at first of *France*, then of *Germany*, and lastly of *England*, served to encrease the swarm in this Country, not only by such as were persecuted at home, but great numbers of peaceable Men, who came here to seek for quiet in their Lives, and safety in their Possessions or Trades; Like those Birds that upon the approach of a rough Winter-season, leave the Countrys where they were born and bred, flye away to some kinder and softer Climate, and never return till the Frosts are past, and the Winds are laid at home.

The invitation these People had, to fix rather in *Holland* than in many better Countrys, seems to have been, at first, the great strength of their Towns, which by their Maritime Scituation, and the low flatness of their Country, can with their Sluces overflow all the ground about them at such distances, as to become inaccessible to any Land-Forces. And this natural strength has been improv'd, especially at *Amsterdam*, by all the Art and Expence that could any ways contribute towards the defence of the place.

Next, was the Constitution of their Government, by which, neither the States-General, nor the Prince, have any power to invade any Man's Person or Property within the precincts of their Cities. Nor could it be fear'd that the Senate of any Town should conspire to any such violence; nor if they did, could they possibly execute it, having no Soldiers in their pay, and the Burgers only being employ'd in the defence of their Towns, and execution of all Civil Justice among them.

These Circumstances gave so great a credit to the Bank of *Amsterdam*; And that was another invitation for People to come, and lodge here what part of their Money they could transport, and knew no way of securing at home. Nor did those People only lodge Moneys here, who came over into the Country; but many more, who never left their own; Though they provided for a retreat, or against a storm, and thought no place so secure as this, nor from whence they might so easily draw their Money into any parts of the World.

Another Circumstance, was, the general Liberty and
Ease, not only in point of Conscience, but all others that
serve to the commodiousness and quiet of life; Every Man
following his own way, minding his own business, and
little enquiring into other Mens; Which, I suppose,
happen'd by so great a concourse of people of several
Nations, different Religions and Customs, as left nothing
strange or new; And by the general humour, bent all upon
Industry, whereas Curiosity is only proper to idle Men.

Besides, it has ever been the great Principle of their State,
running through all their Provinces and Cities, even with
emulation, to make their Country the common refuge of
all miserable Men; From whose protection, hardly any
Alliance, Treaties, or Interests, have ever been able to
divert or remove them. So as, during the great dependence
this State had upon *France*, in the time of *Henry* the Fourth,
all the Persons disgraced at that Court or banisht that
Country, made this their common Retreat; Nor could the
State ever be prevail'd with, by any instances of the *French*
Ambassadors, to refuse them the use and liberty of common
life and air, under the protection of their Government.

This firmness in the State, has been one of the circumstances, that has invited so many unhappy Men out of all
their Neighbourhood, and indeed from most parts of
Europe, to shelter themselves from the blows of Justice, or
of Fortune. Nor indeed does any Country seem so proper
to be made use of upon such occasions, not only in respect
of safety, but as a place that holds so constant and easie
correspondencies with all parts of the World; And whither
any Man may draw whatever Money he has at his disposal
in any other place; Where neither Riches expose Men to
danger, nor Poverty to contempt; But on the contrary,

where Parsimony is honourable, whether it be necessary or no; and he that is forced by his Fortune to live low, may here alone live in fashion, and upon equal terms (in appearance abroad) with the chiefest of their Ministers, and richest of their Merchants: Nor is it easily imagin'd, how great an effect this Constitution among them, may, in course of time, have had upon the encrease both of their People and their Trade.

As the two first invitations of People into this Country, were the strength of their Towns, and nature of their Government; So, two others have grown with the course of time, and progress of their Riches and Power. One is the Reputation of their Government, arising from the observation of the Success of their Arms, the Prudence of their Negotiations, the Steddiness of their Counsels, the Constancy of their Peace and Quiet at home, and the Consideration they hereby arrived at among the Princes and States of Christendom. From all these, Men grew to a general opinion of the Wisdom and Conduct of their State; and of its being establisht upon Foundations, that could not be shaken by any common Accidents, nor consequently in danger of any great or sudden Revolutions; And this is a mighty inducement to industrious People to come and inhabit a Country, who seek not only safety under Laws from Injustice and Oppression, but likewise under the strength and good conduct of a State, from the violence of Foreign Invasions, or of Civil Commotions.

The other, is, the great Beauty of their Country (forced in time, and by the improvements of Industry, in spight of Nature,) which draws every day such numbers of curious and idle persons to see their Provinces, though not to inhabit them. And indeed their Country is a much better

Mistress than a Wife; and where few persons who are well at home, would be content to live; but where none that have time and Money to spare, would not for once be willing to travel; And as *England* shews, in the beauty of the Country, what Nature can arrive at; so does *Holland*, in the number, greatness, and beauty of their Towns, whatever Art can bring to pass. But these and many other matters of Speculation among them, filling the Observations of all common Travellers, shall make no part of mine, whose design is rather to discover the Causes of their Trade and Riches, than to relate the Effects.

Yet it may be noted hereupon, as a piece of wisdom in any Kingdom or State, by the Magnificence of Courts, or of Publick Structures; By encouraging beauty in private Buildings, and the adornment of Towns with pleasant and regular plantations of Trees; By the celebration of some Noble Festivals or Solemnities; By the institution of some great Marts or Fairs; and by the contrivance of any extraordinary and renowned Spectacles, to invite and occasion, as much and as often as can be, the concourse of busie or idle People from the neighbouring or remoter Nations, whose very passage and intercourse is a great encrease of Wealth and of Trade, and a secret incentive of People to inhabit a Country, where Men may meet with equal advantages, and more entertainments of life, than in other places. Such were the *Olympick* and other Games among the *Grecians*; Such the Triumphs, Trophees, and Secular Plays of old *Rome*, as well as the Spectacles exhibited afterwards by the Emperors, with such stupendous effects of Art and Expence, for courting or entertaining the People; Such the Jubilees of new *Rome*; The Justs and Tournaments formerly used in most of the Courts of Christendom;

The Festivals of the more celebrated Orders of Knight-
hood; And in particular Towns, the Carnavals and Faires;
the Kirmeshes, which run through all the Cities of the
Netherlands, and in some of them, with a great deal of
Pageantry, as well as Traffick, being equal baits of Pleasure
and of Gain.

Having thus discover'd, what has laid the great Foundations of their Trade, by the multitude of their People,
which has planted and habituated Industry among them,
and, by that, all sorts of Manufacture; As well as Parsimony,
and thereby general Wealth: I shall enumerate very briefly,
some other Circumstances, that seem, next to these, the
chief Advancers and Encouragers of Trade in their Country.

Low Interest, and dearness of Land, are effects of the
multitude of People, and cause so much Money to lye
ready for all Projects, by which gain may be expected, as
the cutting of Canals, making Bridges and Cawsies,
levelling Downs, and draining Marshes, besides all new
essays at Foreign Trade, which are proposed with any
probability of advantage.

The use of their Banks, which secures Money, and makes
all Payments easie, and Trade quick.

The Sale by Registry, which was introduced here and in
Flanders in the time of *Charles* the Fifth, and makes all
Purchases safe.

The Severity of Justice, not only against all Thefts, but
all Cheats, and Counterfeits of any Publick Bills, (which is
capital among them,) and even against all common Beggars,
who are disposed of either into Workhouses, or Hospitals,
as they are able or unable to labour.

The Convoys of Merchant-Fleets into all parts, even in
time of Peace, but especially into the *Streights*; which give

their Trade Security against many unexpected Accidents, and their Nations Credit abroad, and breeds up Sea-men for their Ships of War.

The lowness of their Customs, and easiness of paying them, which, with the freedom of their Ports, invite both Strangers and Natives to bring Commodities hither, not only as to a Market, but as to a Magazine, where they lodge till they are invited abroad to other and better Markets.

Order and Exactness in managing their Trade, which brings their Commodities in Credit abroad. This was first introduced by severe Laws and Penalties, but is since grown into Custom. Thus there have been above Thirty several Placarts about the manner of curing, pickling, and barrelling, Herrings. Thus all Arms made at *Utrecht* are forfeited, if sold without mark, or marked without Trial. And I observed in their *Indian*-House, that all the pieces of Scarlet, which are sent in great quantities to those parts, are marked with the English Arms, and Inscriptions in English; by which they maintain the credit gain'd to that Commodity, by our former Trade to parts, where 'tis now lost or decay'd.

The Government manag'd either by Men that Trade, or whose Families have risen by it, or who have themselves some Interest going in other Mens Traffique, or, who are born and bred in Towns, the Soul and Being whereof consists wholly in Trade, which makes sure of all favour, that, from time to time, grows necessary, and can be given it by the Government.

The custom of every Towns affecting some particular Commerce or Staple, valuing it self thereupon, and so improving it to the greatest height, as *Flussingue*, by that of the *West-Indies*; *Middleburgh*, of French-Wines; *Terveer*, by the Scotch Staple; *Dort*, by the English Staple and Rhenish Wines; *Rotterdam*, by the English and Scotch Trade at large, and by French Wines; *Leyden*, by the Manufacture of all sorts of Stuffs, Silk, Hair, Gold and Silver; *Haerlem*, by Linen, Mixt-Stuffs, and Flowers; *Delf*, by Beer, and Dutch-Purcelane; *Surdam*, by the built of Ships; *Enchusyen* and *Mazlandsluys*, by Herring-Fishing; *Friezland*, by the *Greenland*-Trade; and *Amsterdam*, by that of the *East-Indies*, *Spain*, and the *Streights*.

The great application of the whole Province to the Fishing-Trade, upon the Coasts of *England* and *Scotland*, which employs an incredible number of Ships and Seamen, and supplies most of the Southern parts of *Europe* with a rich and necessary Commodity.

The last, I shall mention, is, the mighty advance they have made towards engrossing the whole Commerce of the *East-Indies*, by their Successes against the *Portuguesses*, and by their many Wars and Victories against the Natives, whereby they have forced them to Treaties of Commerce, exclusive to all other Nations, and to the admission of Forts to be built upon Streights and Passes, that command the Entrances into the Traffick of such places. This has been atchieved by the multitude of their People and Mariners, that has been able to furnish every year so many great Ships for such Voyages, and to supply the loss of so many Lives, as the changes of Climate have cost, before they learnt the method of living in them: By the vastness of the Stock that has been turn'd wholly to that Trade; And by the conduct and application of the *East-Indy* Company, who have managed it like a Commonwealth, rather than a Trade; And thereby raised a State in the *Indies*, governed indeed

by the Orders of the Company, but otherwise appearing to
those Nations like a Sovereign State, making War and
Peace with their greatest Kings, and able to bring to Sea
Forty or Fifty Men of War, and Thirty thousand Men at
Land, by the modestest computations. The Stock of this
Trade, besides what it turns to in *France, Spain, Italy,* the
Streights, and *Germany,* makes them so great Masters in the
Trade of the Northern parts of *Europe,* as *Muscovy, Poland,
Pomerania,* and all the *Baltique;* where the Spices, that are
an *Indian* Drug, and *European* Luxury, command all the
Commodities of those Countries, which are so necessary to
Life, as their Corn; and to Navigation, as Hemp, Pitch,
Masts, Planks, and Iron.

Thus the Trade of this Country is discovered to be no
effect of common contrivances, of natural dispositions or
scituations, or of trivial accidents; But of a great concurrence
of Circumstances, a long course of Time, force of Orders
and Method, which never before met in the World to such
a degree, or with so prodigious a Success, and perhaps
never will again. Having grown (to sum up all,) from the
scituation of their Country, extended upon the Sea, divided
by two such Rivers as the *Rhyne* and the *Mose,* with the
Vicinity of the *Ems, Weser,* and *Elve;* From the confluence
of people out of *Flanders, England, France,* and *Germany,*
invited by the Strength of their Towns, and by the Constitutions and Credit of their Government; by the Liberty
of Conscience, and security of Life and Goods, (subjected
only to constant Laws;) From general Industry and Parsimony, occasioned by the multitude of People, and smalness
of Country; From cheapness and easiness of Carriage by
convenience of Canals; From low Use, and dearness of
Land, which turn Money to Trade; the Institution of Banks;

Sale by Registry; Care of Convoys; Smalness of Customs; Freedom of Ports; Order in Trade; Interest of Persons in the Government; particular Traffick affected to particular places; Application to the Fishery; and Acquisitions in the *East-Indies*.

It is no constant Rule, That Trade makes Riches; for there may be a Trade, that impoverishes a Nation: As is not going often to Market, that enriches the Country-man; but, on the contrary, if, every time he comes there, he buys to a greater value than he sells, he grows the poorer, the oftner he goes: But the only and certain Scale of Riches, arising from Trade, in a Nation, is the proportion of what is exported for the Consumption of others, to what is imported for their own.

The true ground of this proportion lies in the general Industry and Parsimony of a People, or in the contrary of both. Industry encreases the Native Commodity, either in the product of the Soil, or the Manufactures of the Country, which raises the Stock for Exportation. Parsimony lessens the consumption of their own, as well as of Foreign, Commodities; and not only abates the Importation by the last, but encreases the Exportation by the first; for, of all Native Commodities, the less is consumed in a Country, the more is exported abroad; there being no Commodity, but, at one price or other, will find a Market, which they will be Masters of, who can afford it cheapest; Such are always the most industrious and parsimonious People, who can thrive by Prices, upon which the Lazy and Expensive cannot live.

The vulgar mistake, That Importation of Foreign Wares, if purchased abroad with Native Commodities, and not with Money, does not make a Nation poorer, is but what every Man, that gives himself leisure to think, must immediately rectifie, by finding out, that, upon the end of an Account between a Nation, and all they deal with abroad, whatever the Exportation wants in value, to balance that of the Importation, must of necessity be made up with ready Money.

By this we find out the Foundation of the Riches of *Holland*, as of their Trade by the Circumstances already rehearsed. For never any Country traded so much, and consumed so little: They buy infinitely, but 'tis to sell again, either upon improvement of the Commodity, or at a better Market. They are the great Masters of the *Indian* Spices, and of the *Persian* Silks; but wear plain Woollen, and feed upon their own Fish and Roots. Nay, they sell the finest of their own Cloth to *France*, and buy coarse out of *England* for their own wear. They send abroad the best of their own Butter, into all parts, and buy the cheapest out of *Ireland*, or the North of *England*, for their own use. In short, they furnish infinite Luxury, which they never practise; and traffique in Pleasures, which they never taste.

The Gentlemen and Officers of the Army change their Cloaths and their Modes like their Neighbours. But among the whole body of the Civil Magistrates, the Merchants, the rich Traders, and Citizens in general, the Fashions continue still the same; And others, as constant among the Sea-men and Boors: So that Men leave off their Clothes, only, because they are worn out, and not because they are out of Fashion.

Their great Foreign Consumption is *French*-Wine and *Brandy*; But that may be allow'd them, as the only Reward they enjoy of all their pains, and as that alone, which makes them rich and happy in their voluntary Poverty, who would otherwise seem poor and wretched in their real Wealth. Besides, what they spend in Wine, they save in Corn to make other Drinks, which is bought from Foreign parts. And upon a pressure of their Affairs, we see now for two years together, they have denied themselves even this Comfort, among all their Sorrows, and made up in passive Fortitude, whatever they have wanted in the active.

Thus it happens, that much going constantly out, either in Commodity, or in the Labor of Seafaring-men; and little coming in to be consumed at home; the rest returns in Coin, and fills the Country to that degree, that more Silver is seen in *Holland*, among the common Hands and Purses, than Brass either in *Spain* or in *France*; Though one be so rich in the best Native Commodities, and the other drain all the Treasuries of the *West-Indies*.

By all this account of their Trade and Riches, it will appear, That some of our Maxims are not so certain, as they are current, in our common Politicks. As first, That Example and Encouragement of Excess and Luxury, if employ'd in the consumption of Native Commodities, is of Advantage to Trade: It may be so to that which impoverishes, but is not to that which enriches a Country; and is indeed less prejudicial, if it lie in Native, than in Foreign, Wares. But the Custom, or Humour, of Luxury and Expence, cannot stop at certain Bounds: What begins in Native will proceed in Foreign Commodities; And though the Example arise among idle Persons, yet the Imitation will run into all Degrees, even of those Men by whose Industry the Nation subsists. And besides, the more of our own we spend, the less we shall have to send abroad; and so it will come to pass, that while we drive a vast Trade, yet, by buying much more than we sell, we shall come to be poor: Whereas when we drove a very small Traffique abroad, yet by selling so much more, than we bought, we were very rich in proportion to our Neighbours. This appear'd in *Edward* the Third's time, when we maintain'd so mighty Wars in *France*, and carried our victorious Arms into the heart of *Spain*; Whereas, in the 28th Year of that King's Reign, the Value, and Custom, of all our Exported Commodities, amounted to 294184 *l.*—17*s.*—2*d.* And that of Imported, but to 38970*l.*—03*s.*—06*d.* So, as there must have enter'd that Year into the Kingdom in Coin, or Bullion, (or else have grown a Debt to the Nation) 255214*l.*—13*s.*—08*d.* And yet we then carry'd out our Wools unwrought, and brought in a great part of our Cloaths from *Flanders*.

Another common Maxim is, That if, by any Foreign Invasion, or Servitude, the State, and consequently the Trade, of *Holland*, should be ruin'd, the last would of course fall to our share in *England*. Which is no consequence: For it would certainly break into several pieces, and shift, either to us, to *Flanders*, to the *Hans-Towns*, or any other parts, according as the most of those circumstances should any where concur to invite it, (and the likest to such,) as appear to have formerly drawn it into *Holland*, by so mighty a confluence of People, and so general a vein of Industry and Parsimony among them. And whoever pretends to equal their growth in Trade and Riches, by other ways than such as are already enumerated, will prove, I doubt, either to deceive, or to be deceived.

A third is, That if that State were reduced to great Extremities, so as to become a Province to some greater Power, they would chuse our Subjection rather than any other; or those, at least, that are the Maritime, and the richest of the Provinces. But it will be more reasonably concluded, from all the former Discourses, That though they may be divided by absolute Conquests, they will never divide themselves by consent, but all fall one way, and, by common Agreement, make the best Terms they can for their Country, as a Province, if not as a State: And before they come to such an extremity, they will first seek to be admitted, as a *Belgick*-Circle, in the Empire, (which they were of old;) and thereby receive the protection of that Mighty Body, which (as far as great and smaller things may be compar'd) seems the likest their own State in its main Constitutions, but especially in the Freedom or Sovereignty of the Imperial Cities. And this I have often heard their Ministers speak of, as their last refuge, in case of being threatned by too strong and fatal a Conjuncture.

And if this should happen, the Trade of the Provinces would rather be preserved or encreased, than any way broken or destroy'd by such an alteration of their State, because the Liberties of the Country would continue what they are, and the Security would be greater than now it is.

The last I will mention, is of another vein; That if the Prince of *Orange* were made Sovereign of their Country, though by Foreign Arms, he would be a great Prince, because this now appears to be so great a State. Whereas, on the contrary, those Provinces would soon become a very mean Country. For such a Power must be maintain'd by force, as it would be acquir'd, and as indeed all absolute Dominion must be in those Provinces. This would raise general Discontents; and those, perpetual Seditions among the Towns, which would change the Orders of the Country, endanger the Property of Private Men, and shake the Credits and Safety of the Government: Whenever this should happen, the People would scatter, Industry would faint, Banks would dissolve, and Trade would decay to such a degree, as probably, in course of time, their very Digues would be no longer maintained by the Defences of a weak People against so furious an Invader; but the Sea would break in upon their Land, and leave their chiefest Cities to be Fisher-Towns, as they were of old.

Without any such great Revolutions, I am of opinion, That Trade has, for some years ago, past its Meridian, and begun sensibly to decay among them: Whereof there seem to be several Causes; as first, the general Application, that so many other Nations have made to it, within these two or three and twenty years. For since the Peace of *Munster*, which restored the quiet of Christendom in 1648, not only *Sueden* and *Denmark*, but *France* and *England*, have more particularly, than ever before, busied the Thoughts and Counsels of their several Governments, as well as the Humours of their People, about the matters of Trade.

Nor has this happen'd without good degrees of Success; though Kingdoms of such extent, that have other and Nobler Foundations of Greatness, cannot raise Trade to such a pitch as this little State, which had no other to build upon; no more than a Man, who has a fair and plentiful Estate, can fall to Labour and Industry, like one that has nothing else to trust to for the support of his Life. But however, all these Nations have come of late to share largely with them; and there seem to be grown too many Traders for Trade in the World, so as they can hardly live one by another. As in a great populous Village, the first Grocer, or Mercer, that sets up among them, grows presently rich, having all the Custom; till another, encouraged by his success, comes to set up by him, and share in his

Gains; at length so many fall to the Trade, that nothing is got by it; and some must give over, or all must break.

Not many Ages past, *Venice* and *Florence* possest all the Trade of *Europe*; The last by their Manufactures; But the first by their Shipping: And the whole Trade of *Persia* and the *Indies*, whose Commodities were brought (Those by Land, and These by the *Arabian*-Sea,) to *Egypt*, from whence they were fetcht by the *Venetian* Fleets, and dispersed into most of the parts of *Europe*: And in those times we find the whole Trade of *England* was driven by *Venetians*, *Florentines*, and *Lombards*. The *Easterlings*, who were the Inhabitants of the *Hans*-Towns, as *Dantzic*, *Lubeick*, *Hamburgh*, and others upon that Coast, fell next into Trade, and managed all that of these Northern parts for many years, and brought it first down to *Bruges*, and from thence to *Antwerp*. The first Navigations of the *Portuguesses* to the *East-Indies* broke the greatness of the *Venetian* Trade, and drew it to *Lisbon*; And the Revolt of the *Netherlands*, that of *Antwerp* to *Holland*. But in all this time, The other and greater Nations of *Europe* concern'd themselves little in it; Their Trade was War; Their Counsels and Enterprises were busied in the quarrels of the *Holy Land*, or in those between the Popes and the Emperors (both of the same Forge, engaging all Christian Princes, and ending in the greatness of the Ecclesiastical State throughout Christendom:) Sometimes in the mighty Wars between *England* and *France*, between *France* and *Spain*: The more general, between *Christian* and *Turks*; Or more particular quarrels between lesser and Neighbouring-Princes. In short, the Kingdoms and Principalities were in the World like the Noblemen and Gentlemen in a Country; The Free-States and Cities, like the Merchants and Traders: These at first despised by the others; The others serv'd and rever'd by them; till by the various course of Events in the World, some of these came to grow Rich and Powerful by Industry and Parsimony; And some of the others, Poor by War and by Luxury: Which made the Traders begin to take upon them, and carry it like Gentlemen; and the Gentlemen begin to take a fancy of falling to Trade. By this short account it will appear no wonder, either that particular places grew so Rich, and so Mighty, while they alone enjoyed almost the general Trade of the World; nor why not only the Trade in *Holland*, but the advantage of it in general, should seem to be lessen'd by so many that share it.

Another cause of its decay in that State, may be, that, by the mighty progress of their *East-India* Company, the Commodities of that Country are grown more than these parts of the World can take off; and consequently, the Rates of them must needs be lessened, while the Charge is encreas'd by the great Wars, the Armies, and Forts, necessary to maintain, or extend, the Acquisitions of that Company, in the *Indies*. For, instead of Five, or Six *East-India* Ships, which used to make the Fleet of the Year, they are now risen to Eighteen or Twenty, (I think Two and Twenty came in one Year to the *United Provinces*.) This is the reason, why the particular persons of that Company in *Holland*, make not so great advantage of the same Stock, as those of ours do in *England*; Though their Company be very much richer, and drives a far greater Trade than ours, which is exhausted by no charge of Armies, or Forts, or Ships of War: And this is the reason, that the *Dutch* are forced to keep so long and so much of those Commodities in their Magazines here, and to bring them out, only as the

Markets call for them, or are able to take off; And why they bring so much less from the *Indies*, than they were able to do, if there were vent enough here: As I remember one of their Sea-men, newly landed out of their *East-Indy* Fleet, in the Year 69, upon discourse in a Boat between *Delf* and *Leyden*, said, he had seen, before he came away, three heaps of Nutmegs burnt at a time, each of which, was more than a small Church could hold, which he pointed at in a Village that was in sight.

Another Cause may be, the great cheapness of Corn, which has been for these dozen Years, or more, general in all these parts of *Europe*, and which has a very great influence upon the Trade of *Holland*. For a great vent of *Indian* Commodities (at least the Spices, which are the gross of them) used to be made into the Northern parts of *Europe*, in exchange for Corn, while it was taken off at good rates by the Markets of *Flanders*, *England*, *France*, *Spain*, or *Italy*; In all which Countrys it has of late years gone so low, as to discourage the Import of so great quantities, as used to come from *Poland* and *Prussia*, and other parts of the North. Now the less value those Nations receive for Corn, the less they are able to give for Spice, which is a great loss to the *Dutch* on both sides, lessening the vent of their *Indian* Ware in the Northern, and the Traffick of Corn in the Southern, parts. The cause of this great cheapness of Corn seems to be, not so much a course of plentiful and seasonable years, as the general Peace that has been in *Europe* since the year 59 or 60; by which so many Men and so much Land have been turned to Husbandry, that were before employ'd in the Wars, or lay wasted by them in all the Frontier-Provinces of *France* and *Spain*, as well as throughout *Germany*, before the Peace of

Munster; and in *England*, during the Actions or Consequences of a Civil War; And Plenty grows not to a height,
but by the Succession of several peacefull as well as seasonable Years.

The last Clause I will mention, is the mighty enlarge-
ment of the City of *Amsterdam*, by that which is called the
New Town; The Extent whereof is so spacious, and the
Buildings of so much greater Beauty and Cost than the
Old, that it must have employ'd a vast proportion of that
Stock which in this City was before wholly turned to
Trade. Besides, there seems to have been growing on for
these later years, a greater Vie of Luxury and Expence
among many of the Merchants of that Town, than was ever
formerly known; Which was observed and complained of,
as well as the enlargement of their City, by some of the
wisest of their Ministers, while I resided among them, who
designed some Regulations by Sumptuary Laws; As knowing the very Foundations of their Trade would soon be
undermined, if the habitual Industry, Parsimony, and
Simplicity of their People, came to be over-run by Luxury,
Idleness, and Excess. However it happen'd, I found it
agreed by all the most diligent and circumspect Enquiries I
could make, that in the years 69 and 70, there was hardly
any Foreign Trade among them, besides that of the *Indies*,
by which the Traders made the returns of their Money,
without loss; and none, by which the common Gain was
above Two or Three in the Hundred. So, as it seems to be
with Trade, as with the Sea, (its Element,) that has a certain
pitch, above which, it never rises in the highest Tides; And
begins to Ebb, as soon as ever it ceases to Flow; And ever
loses ground in one place, proportionable to what it gains
in another.

CHAPTER VII

Of their Forces and Revenues

The Strength, and Forces, of a Kingdom, or State, were measured in former Ages, by the Numbers of Native and Warlike Subjects, which they could draw into the Field, upon any War with their Neighbours. National Quarrels were decided by National Armies, not by Stipendiary Forces, (raised with Money, or maintained by constant Pay.) In the several Kingdoms and Principalities of *Europe*, the Bodies of their Armies were composed, as they are still in *Poland*, of the Nobility and Gentry, who were bound to attend their Princes to the Wars, with certain numbers of Armed Men, according to the tenure and extent of the several Lordships, and Lands, they held of the Crown: Where these were not proportionable to the occasion, the rest were made up of Subjects drawn together by love of their Prince, or their Country; By desire of Conquest and Spoils, or necessity of defence; Held together by Allegiance or Religion; And Spirited by Honour, Revenge, or Avarice (not of what they could get from their Leaders, but from their Enemies.) A Battel or two, fairly fought, decided a War; and a War ended the quarrel of an Age, and either lost or gain'd the Cause or Country contended for: Till the change of Times and Accidents brought it to a new decision; Till the Virtues and Vices of Princes made them stronger or weaker, either in the love and Obedience of their People, or in such Orders and Customs as render'd their Subjects more or less Warlike or Effeminate. Standing-Forces or Guards in constant pay, were no where used by lawful

Princes in their Native or Hereditary Countrys, but only by Conquerors in subdued Provinces, or Usurpers at home; And were a defence only against Subjects, not against Enemies.

These Orders seem first to have been changed in *Europe* by the two States of *Venice* and *Holland*; Both of them small in Territories at Land, and those extended in Frontier upon powerful Neighbours: Both of them weak in number of Native Subjects; and those less warlike at Land, by turning so much to Trafick, and to Sea: But both of them mighty in Riches and Trade; Which made them endeavour to balance their Neighbours strength in Native Subjects, by Foreign Stipendiary Bands; And to defend their Frontiers by the Arts of Fortification, and strength of places, which might draw out a War into length by Sieges, when they durst not venture it upon a Battel; And so make it many times determine by force of Money, rather than of Arms. This forced those Princes, who frontier'd upon these States to the same provisions; Which have been encreast by the perpetual course of Wars, upon the Continent of *Europe*, ever since the rise of this State, until the Peace of the *Pirenees*, between Princes bordering one upon the other; and so, ready for sudden Inroads or Invasions.

The Force therefore of these Provinces is to be measur'd, not by the number or dispositions of their Subjects, but by the strength of their Shipping, and standing-Troops, which they constantly maintain, even in time of peace; And by the numbers of both which, they have been able to draw into the Field, and to Sea, for support of a War: By their constant Revenue to maintain the first; And by the temporary charge, they have been able to furnish, for supply of the other.

I will not enumerate their Frontier Towns, (which is a common Theme,) or the Forces necessary for the Garrisons of them. Nor the Nature and variety of their Taxes and Impositions, though I have an exact List of them by me, expressing the several Kinds, Rates, and Proportions, upon every Province and Town; But this would swell a Discourse, with a great deal of tedious matter, and to little purpose. I shall therefore be content only to observe, what I have informed myself of their Forces, and Revenues in general, from persons among them, the best able to give that account.

The ordinary Revenue of this State, consists, either in what is levied in the conquered Towns, and Country of *Brabant*, *Flanders*, or the *Rhine*; Which is wholly administred by the Council of State: Or else, the ordinary Fonds, which the Seven Provinces provide every Year, according to their several proportions, upon the petition of the Council of State, and Computation of the Charge of the ensuing year, given in by them to the States-General. And this Revenue commonly amounts to about One and twenty Millions of Gilders a Year; Every Million making about Ninety thousand pounds *Sterling*, intrinsick value.

The chief Fonds out of which this rises, Is the Excise and the Customs: The first is great, and so general, that I have heard it observed at *Amsterdam*, That, when in a Tavern, a certain Dish of Fish is eaten with the usual Sawce, above Thirty several Excises are paid, for what is necessary to that small Service. The last are low and easie, and applied particularly to the Admiralty.

Out of this Revenue is supplied the Charge of the whole Milice, of all Publique Officers of the State, and

Ambassadors, or Ministers abroad, and the Interest of about Thirteen Millions owing by the States-General.

The Standing-Forces in the Year 70, upon so general a Peace, and after all Reformations, were Twenty Six Thousand two Hundred Men, in Ten Regiments of Horse, consisting of Fifty Troops; And Nineteen of Foot, consisting of Three Hundred and Eighty Companies. The constant charge of these Forces stood them in Six Millions One Hundred and Nineteen Thousand Gilders a year.

Their Admiralties, in time of Peace, maintain between Thirty and Forty Men of War, employ'd in the several Convoys of their Merchants Fleets, in a Squadron of Eight or Ten Ships to attend the *Algerines* and other *Corsaires* in the *Mediterranean*; And some always lying ready in their Havens for any sudden accidents or occasions of the State. The common Expence of the Admiralties in this Equipage, and the built of Ships, is about six Millions a year.

Besides the Debt of the Generalty, the Province of *Holland* owes about Sixty Five Millions, for which they pay Interest at Four in the Hundred; But with so great ease and exactness both in Principal and Interest, that no Man ever demands it twice; they might take up whatever Money they desired. Whoever is admitted to bring in his Money, takes it for a great deal of favour; And when they pay off any part of the Principal, those, it belongs to, receive it with Tears, not knowing how to dispose of it to Interest, with such Safety and Ease. And the common Revenue of particular Men lies much in the Cantores, either of the Generality, or the several Provinces, which are the Registries of these publique Debts.

Of the several Imposts, and Excises, those that are upon certain, and immovable Possessions (as Houses and Lands) are collected by the Magistrates of the several places, and by them paid in to the Receivers, because both the number and value of them are constant, and easily known. Those which arise out of uncertain Consumptions, are all set out to Farm; and to him that bids most, some every three Months, some every six, and some yearly.

The Collection, Receipt, and Distribution of all Publique Monies, are made, without any Fee to Officers, who receive certain constant Salaries from the State, which they dare not encrease by any private practises, or Extortions; So, whoever has a Bill of any publique Debt, has so much ready Money in his Coffers, being paid certainly at call, without charge, or trouble; and assign'd over in any payment, like the best Bill of Exchange.

The extraordinary Revenue is, when upon some great occasions, or Wars, the Generality agrees to any extraordinary Contributions; As sometimes the Hundredth penny of the Estates of all the Inhabitants; Pole, or Chimney-money; Or any other Subsidies, and Payments, according as they can agree, and the occasions require; which have sometimes reached so far, as even to an Imposition upon every Man that travels in the common ways of their Country, by Boat, or in a Coach; in Wagon, or on Horseback.

By all these means, in the first Year of the *English* War, in 1665; There were raised in the Provinces, Forty Millions, of which Twenty two in the Province of *Holland*. And upon the Bishop of *Munster's* invading them, at the same time by Land, they had in the Year 66, above Threescore thousand Land-men in Pay; And a Fleet of above an Hundred Men of War at Sea.

The Greatness of this Nation, at that time, seems justly

to have raised the Glory of ours; which, during the years 65 and 66, maintained a War, not only against this Powerful State, but against the Crowns of *France* and *Denmark*, in conjunction with them: And all, at a time, when this Kingdom was forced to struggle at home with the calamitous Effects of a raging Plague, that, in Three months of the first year, swept away incredible numbers of People; and of a prodigious Fire, that, in Three days of the second, laid in Ashes that Ancient and Famous City of *LONDON*, (the Heart and Center of our Commerce and Riches,) consuming the greatest part of its Buildings, and an immense proportion of its Wealth. Yet, in the mid'st of these fatal Accidents, those two Summers were renowned with Three Battels of the mightiest Fleets that ever met upon the Ocean; whereof Two were determined by entire and unquestion'd Victories, and pursuit of our Enemies into their very Havens. The Third having begun by the unfortunate division of our Fleet, with the odds of Ninety of their Ships against Fifty of ours; And in spight of such disadvantages, having continued, or been renewed for three days together (wherein we were every Morning the Aggressors,) ended at last by the equal and mutual Weakness or Weariness of both Sides, the maims of Ships and Tackling, with want of Powder and Ammunition; Having left undecided the greatest Action that will perhaps appear upon Record of any Story. And in this Battel, *Monsieur de Wit* confest to me, That we gain'd more Honour to our Nation, and to the invincible Courage of our Sea-men, than by the other two Victories. That he was sure, their Men could never have been brought on the two following days, after the disadvantages of the first; And he believed no other Nation was capable of it, but Ours.

I will not judge, how we came to fail of a glorious Peace in the Six Months next succeeding, after the fortune of our last Victory, and with the Honour of the War: But as any rough Hand can break a Bone, whereas much Art and Care are required to set it again, and restore it to its first strength and proportion; So 'tis an easie part in a Minister of State, to engage a War; but 'tis given to few to know the times, and find the ways, of making Peace. Yet when after the sensible events of an unfortunate Negligence, an indifferent Treaty was concluded at *Breda* in 67; Within Six Months following, by an Alliance with this State in *January*, 1668. (which was received with incredible Joy and Applause among them,) His Majesty became the unquestioned Arbiter of all the Affairs of Christendom; Made a Peace between the two Great Crowns, at *Aix-la-Chapelle*, which was avowed by all the World, to be perfectly His Own; And was received with equal Applause of Christian Princes abroad, and of his Subjects at home; And for three years succeeding, by the unshaken Alliance and Dependance of the United States, His Majesty remained Absolute Master of the Peace of Christendom, and in a posture of giving Bounds to the greatest, as well as Protection to the weakest, of his Neighbours.

CHAPTER VIII

The Causes of their Fall in 1672

It must be avowed, That as This State, in the course and progress of its Greatness for so many years past, has shined like a Comet; So in the Revolutions of this last Summer, It seem'd to fall like a Meteor, and has equally amazed the World by the one and the other: When we consider such a Power and Wealth, as was related in the last Chapter, to have fallen in a manner prostrate within the space of one Month: So many Frontier Towns, renowned in the Sieges and Actions of the *Spanish* Wars, enter'd like open Villages by the *French* Troops, without defence or almost denial: Most of them without any blows at all, and all of them with so few: Their great Rivers, that were esteemed an invincible security to the Provinces of *Holland* and *Utrecht*, passed with as much ease, and as small resistances, as little Fords: And in short, the very hearts of a Nation so valiant of old, against *Rome*, so obstinate against *Spain*, now subdued, and, in a manner, abandoning all before their Danger appeared: We may justly have our recourse to the secret and fixed periods of all Human Greatness, for the account of such a Revolution: Or rather, to the unsearchable Decrees, and unresistable force, of Divine Providence; Though it seems not more impious to question it, than to measure it by our Scale; Or reduce the issues and Motions of that Eternal Will and Power, to a conformity with what is esteemed Just, or Wise, or Good, by the usual Consent, or the narrow comprehension, of poor Mortal Men.

But, as in the search, and consideration, even of things natural and common, our Talent, I fear, is to Talk rather than to Know; So we may be allowed to Enquire and Reason upon all things, while we do not pretend to Certainty, or call that Undeniable Truth, which is every day denied by Ten thousand; Nor those Opinions Unreasonable, which we know to be held by such, as we allow to be Reasonable Men. I shall therefore set down such circumstances, as to me seem most evidently to have conspired in this Revolution; leaving the Causes less discernable, to the search of more discerning Persons.

And first, I take their vast Trade, which was an occasion of their Greatness, to have been One likewise of their Fall, by having wholly diverted the Genius of their Native Subjects, and Inhabitants, from Arms, to Traffique, and the Arts of Peace; Leaving the whole fortune of their later Wars, to be managed, by Foreign and Mercenary Troops; which much abased the Courage of their Nation, (as was observed in another Chapter,) and made the Burghers of so little moment towards the defence of their Towns; Whereas, in the famous Sieges of *Harlem*, *Alcmar*, and *Leyden*, They had made such brave and fierce defences, as broke the Heart of the *Spanish* Armies, and the fortune of their Affairs.

Next, was the Peace of *Munster*, which had left them now, for above Twenty years, too secure of all Invasions, or Enemies at Land; And so turn'd their whole application to the strength of their Forces at Sea; Which have been since exercised with two *English* Wars in that time, and enlivened with the small yearly Expeditions into the *Streights* against the *Algerines*, and other *Corsairs* of the *Mediterranean*.

Another was, their too great Parsimony, in Reforming so many of their best Foreign Officers and Troops, upon the Peace of *Munster*; whose Valour and Conduct had been so great occasions of inducing *Spain* to the Counsels and Conclusions of that Treaty.

But the greatest of all others, that concurr'd to weaken, and indeed break, the strength of their Land-Milice, was, the alteration of their State, which happen'd by the *Perpetual Edict* of *Holland*, and *West-Friezland*, upon the death of the last Prince of *Orange*, for exclusion of the Power of Stadtholder in their Province, or at least the separation of it from the Charge of Captain-General. Since that time, the main design, and application of those Provinces, has been, to work out, by degrees, all the old Officers, both Native and Foreign, who had been formerly Sworn to the Prince of *Orange*, and were still thought affectionate to the Interest of that Family; And to fill the Commands of their Army, with the Sons, or Kinsmen, of Burgomasters, and other Officers, or Deputies in the State, whom they esteemed sure to the Constitutions of their Popular Government, and good enough for an Age, where they saw no appearance of Enemy at Land to attaque them.

But the Humour of Kindness to the young Prince, both in the People, and Army, was not to be dissolved, or dispersed, by any Medicines, or Operations, either of Rigor or Artifice; But grew up insensibly, with the Age of the Prince[1], ever presaging some Revolution in the State, when he should come to the years of aspiring, and managing the general Affections of the People: Being a Prince, who joyned to the great Qualities of his Royal Blood, the popular Virtues of his Country; Silent and Thoughtful;

[1] Crevit occulto velut arbor aevo, Fama Marcelli.

Given to hear, and to enquire; Of a sound and steddy Understanding; Much firmness in what he once resolves, or once denies; Great Industry and Application to his Business; Little to his Pleasures: Piety in the Religion of his Country, but with Charity to others; Temperance unusual to his Youth, and to the Climate; Frugal in the common management of his Fortune, and yet magnificent upon occasion: Of great Spirit and Heart, aspiring to the Glory of Military Actions, with strong Ambition to grow Great, but rather by the Service, than the Servitude, of his Country. In short, A Prince of many Virtues, without any appearing mixture of Vice.

In the *English* War, begun the year 65. the States disbanded all the *English* Troops, that were then left in their Service, dispersing the Officers and Soldiers of our Nation, who staid with them, into other Companies, or Regiments, of their own. After the *French* Invasion of *Flanders*, and the strict Alliance between *England* and *Holland* in 68. they did the same by all the *French* that were remaining in their Service. So as the several Bodies of these two Nations, which had ever the greatest part in the Honour and Fortune of their Wars, were now wholly dissolved, and their standing-Milice composed in a manner, all of their own Natives, enervated by the long Uses and Arts of Traffique, and of Peace.

But they were too great a Match for any of the smaller Princes their Neighbours in *Germany*; And too secure of any danger from *Spain*, by the knowledge of their Forces, as well as Dispositions; And being strictly Allied both with *England* and *Sueden*, in two several Defensive Leagues, and in one common Triple Alliance; They could not foresee any danger from *France*, who, they thought, would never have the Courage, or Force, to enter the Lists with so mighty Confederates; and who were sure of a Conjunction, whenever they pleased, both with the Emperor and *Spain*.

Besides, They knew that *France* could not attaque them, without passing through *Flanders*, or *Germany*: They were sure *Spain* would not suffer it through the first, if they were backt in opposing it, as foreseeing the inevitable loss of *Flanders*, upon that of *Holland*: And they could hardly believe, the passage should be yielded by a *German* Prince, contrary to the express Will and Intentions of the Emperor, as well as the common Interests of the Empire: So that they hoped the War would, at least, open in their Neighbours Provinces, for whose Defence they resolved to employ the whole Force of their State. And would have made a mighty resistance, if the Quarrel had begun at any other Doors, but their own.

They could not imagine a Conjunction between *England* and *France*, for the ruine of their State; For, being unacquainted with our Constitutions, they did not foresee, how we should find our Interest in it, and measured all States, by that which They esteemed to be their Interest. Nor could they believe, that other Princes and States of *Europe* would suffer such an addition to be made to the Power of *France*, as a Conquest of *Holland*.

Besides these publick Considerations, there were others particular to the Factions among them; And some of their Ministers were neither forward nor supple enough to endeavour the early breaking, or diverting, such Conjunctures, as threatned them; Because they were not without hopes, they might end in renewing their broken Measures with *France*; Which those of the Commonwealth-Party were more enclin'd to, by foreseeing the influence that their

Alliances with *England* must needs have in time, towards the restoring of the Prince of *Orange's* Authority: And they thought at the worst, that whenever a pinch came, they could not fail of a safe bargain in one Market or other, having so vast a Treasure ready to employ upon any good occasion.

These Considerations made them commit three fatal Oversights in their Foreign Negotiations: For they made an Alliance with *England*, without engaging a Confidence and Friendship: They broke their Measures with *France*, without closing new ones with *Spain*: And they reckon'd upon the Assistances of *Sweden*, and their Neighbour-Princes of *Germany*, without making them sure by Subsidiary Advances, before a War began.

Lastly, The Prince of *Orange* was approaching the Two and twentieth year of his Age, which the States of *Holland* had, since their Alliance with His Majesty in 1668, ever pretended, should be the time of advancing him to the Charge of Captain-General, and Admiral of their Forces, though without that of Stadtholder. But the nearer they drew to this period, which was like to make a new Figure in their Government; the more desirous some of their Ministers seemed, either to decline, or to restrain, it. On the other side, the Prince grew confident upon the former Promises, or, at least, Intimations, of *Holland*, and the concurring dispositions of the other Six Provinces to his advancement: And his Party, spirited by their hopes, and the great Qualities, of this young Prince, (now grown ripe for Action, and for Enterprize,) resolved to bring this point to a sudden decision; Against which, the other Party prepared, and united all their Defences; So, as this strong Disease, that had been so long working in the very Bowels of the State, seem'd just upon its *Crisis*; When a Conjunction of Two Mighty Kings brought upon them a sudden and furious Invasion by Land and Sea, at the same time, by a Royal Fleet, of above Fourscore Ships; and an Army, of as many thousand Men.

When the States saw this Cloud ready to break upon them, (after a long belief that it would blow over,) They began, not only to provide shelter at home, with their usual vigor; but to look out for it abroad, though both too late. Of the Princes that were their Allies, or concern'd in their danger, Such as were far off could not be in time; The nearer were unwilling to share in a danger they were not enough prepar'd for; Most were content to see the Pride of this State humbled; Some, the Injuries, they had received from them, revenged; Many would have them mortified, that would not have them destroyed; And so all resolved to leave them to weather the Storm, as they could, for one *Campania*; Which, they did not believe, could go far towards their ruin, considering the greatness of their Riches, number of their Force, and strength of their Places.

The State, in the mean time, had encreased their Troops to Seventy thousand Men, and had begun to repair the Fortifications of their Frontier Towns: But so great a length of their Country lay open to the *French* Invasion, by the Territories of *Colen* and *Liege*; And to the Bishop of *Munster*, (their inveterate Enemy,) by *Westphalia*, that they knew not where to expect, or provide against, the first danger: And while they divided their Forces and Endeavours towards the securing of so many Garisons, they provided for none to any purpose but *Maestricht*; Which the *French* left behind them, and fell in upon the Towns of the *Rhine*, and the Heart of their Provinces.

Besides, Those Ministers, who had still the direction of Affairs, bent their chief application to the Strength and Order of their Fleet, rather than of their Army: Whether more peckt at *England* than *France*, upon the War, and manner of entring into it; Or, believing that a Victory at Sea would be the way to a Peace with this Crown; Or, hoping their Towns would not fall so fast, but that, before three or four were lost, the business at Sea would be decided; Or perhaps content, that some ill Successes should attend the Prince of *Orange* at his first entrance upon the Command of their Armies, and thereby contribute to their Designs of restraining the Authority, while they were forced to leave him the Name, of Captain-General. This, indeed, was not likely to fail, considering the ill constitution of their old Army, the hasty Levies of their new, and the heighth of the Factions now broken out in the State; Which left both the Towns and the Troops in suspence, under whose Banners they fought, and by whose Orders they were to be govern'd, the Prince's, or the States.

There happen'd, at the same time, an accident unusual to their Climate, which was a mighty Drowth in the beginning of the Summer, that left their waters fordable in places, where they used to be navigable for Boats of greatest burthen. And this gave them more trouble and distraction in the defence, as their Enemies more facility in the passage, of those great Rivers, which were esteemed no small security of their Country.

And in this posture were the Affairs of this Common-wealth, when the War broke out, with those fatal Events, that must needs attend any Kingdom, or State, where the violence of a Foreign Invasion happens to meet with the distracted estate of a Domestique Sedition or Discontent, which, like ill Humours in a Body, make any small wound dangerous, and a great one mortal. They were still a great Body, but without their usual Soul; They were a State, but it was of the *Dis-united Provinces*. Their Towns were without Order; Their Burgers without Obedience; Their Soldiers without Discipline; And all without Heart: Whereas, in all Sieges, The Hearts of Men defend the Walls, and not Walls the Men: And, indeed, it was the Name of *England*, joyning in the War against them, that broke their Hearts, and contributed more to the loss of so many Towns, and so much Country, than the Armies of *Munster*, or of *France*. So that, upon all circumstances consider'd, it seems easier to give an account, what it was that lost them so much, than what sav'd them the rest.

No Man at play sees a very great Game, either in his own, or another's, Hand, unexpectedly lost, but he is apt to consider, whether it could have been saved, and how it ought to have been play'd. The same Enquiry will be natural upon the Fall of this State, and very difficult to resolve.

After the mighty growth of the *French*, and decay of the *Spanish* Power, which drew on the Invasion of *Flanders* in 1667. This State had a very hard Game to play; Either they must see *Flanders* wholly lost, and *France* grown to confine upon them, (whom they liked as an Ally, but dreaded as a Neighbour;) Or else, they must join with *France* to divide *Flanders* between them; But they knew what it was to share with the Lion: Or, they must joyn with *Spain* to defend *Flanders* against *France*, that is, with their old Enemy, against their old Friend: Or lastly, They must joyn with *England* for the defence of *Flanders*; Neither breaking with *France*, nor closing with *Spain*; and frame an Arbitrage, but

of somthing a rough nature; rather prescribing than mediating a Peace, and threatning a War upon that Crown that
refused it.

They chose the last, and wisely, as all men thought;
But though this Alliance was happily planted, yet it was
unhappily cultivated, and so the Fruit came to fall, and the
Root to wither upon the first change of seasons, in such a
manner, and to such a degree, as we have lately seen.
Whether they could have prevented a Conjunction of
England with *France*, shall be no part of my Subject; For I
pretend not to know, or to tell, Secrets of State; and intend
these, not for the Observations of an Ambassador, but of a
private man as I am, and such as any Gentleman might
easily have made, who had resided above two years, as I
did, in *Holland*; and had been, as I was, a little enclined to
observe. I shall only say, That the Conjunction of *England*
with *France* was to this State, like one of those Diseases,
which, the Physicians say, are hard to discern, while they
are easie to cure; but when once they come to be plainly
discovered, they are past remedy.

But, as *Holland* had ever defended it self against *Spain*,
by *England* and *France*; So it ought to have done against
France, by *England* and *Spain*, and provided early against
their own danger, as well as that of *Flanders*, by improving
and advancing their Confederate League with *England* and
Sweden, into a strict Defensive-Alliance with *Spain*, as a
Principal in the League. And by agreeing with that Crown,
to furnish between them some constant Subsidiary Payments to *Sweden*, for the support of their standing-Forces,
even in time of Peace. This was the desire of *Spain*, the
Interest of all that meant to secure the Peace of Christendom; and the opinion of some of the *Dutch* Ministers,

though not of the Chiefest, till it was too late: And the omission of This, was the greatest fault ever committed in their Politicks; and proceeded in a great measure from their ancient animosity to *Spain*; Which as it was the beginning, so, by this effect, it almost prov'd the end of their State.

When the War began in the mid'st of the Conjunctures related, 'Tis hard to say, what could have defended them; But as men in a Town, threatned with a mighty Siege, abandon their Suburbs, and slight those Out-works which are either weak of themselves, or not well defensible for want of Men; and resolve onely to make good those Posts which they are able fully to man, and easily to relieve; because the loss of every small Out-work does not only weaken the Number, but sink the Courage, of the Garison within.

So this State, which came to be in a manner besieged by the mighty and numerous Armies of *France* and of *Munster*, ought, in my opinion, to have left themselves but three Out-works to maintain; (I mean, three Posts standing without the Lines, that enclosed the main Body of their Provinces:) These should have been *Maestricht, Wesel* and *Coeverden.* They should have slighted all the rest of their places, that lay without these upon the *Rhine*, or in *Overyssel*; and drawn the Men into these Towns, so as to have left them rather like Camps, than Garisons, that is, Eight thousand Foot, and two thousand Horse in *Maestricht*, as many in *Wesel*, and half the number in *Coeverden*, if the place would contain them; if not, they might have formed and fortified a Camp, with something a greater number, upon the next Pass into *Friezland* and *Groninguen.*

Of the rest of their Horse, (which were, I suppose, about Five thousand) with at least Fifteen thousand Foot, they

should have formed a great standing Camp, within their
Rivers, somewhere near *Arnhem*; Fortifi'd it with Canon,
and all the Art that could be; Furnisht it with the greatest
care, and Plenty of Provisions. The remainder of their
Infantry would have been enough for the rest of their
Garisons; Of which the Towns upon the *Yssel, Does-
burgh, Zutphen, Daventer, and Swoll*, would have been in
a manner flankt (though at some distance) by the strong
Garisons of *Wesel* and *Coeverden*; and breasted by the main
Camp.

If, with this disposition of their Forces, they had provided
well for the strength and defence of *Skinksconce, Nimmeguen* and *Grave*, (which would likewise have lien all
within the cover of these out-Posts:) They might, for
ought I know, have expected the War without losing the
heart and steddiness of their Counsels, and not without
probability of making a defence worthy the former Greatness and Atchievements of their State.

For a Siege of *Maestricht* or *Wesel* (so garrison'd and
resolutely defended,) might not onely have amused, but
endanger'd, the *French* Armies; As *Coeverden* might have
done that of *Munster*. The resistance of one of these Towns
would have encreased the strength of all the rest: For the
Fortune of Battels, and Sieges, turns upon the hearts of
men, as they are more or less capable of general Confidences
or Fears, which are very much raised by Accidents and
Opinions. It would not have been within any common
Rules, to march so far into the Country, as to attacque the
Burse or *Breda, Nimmeguen* or *Grave*, leaving such Camps
behind, as those at *Wesel* and *Maestricht*, and having so
much a greater before them, as that about *Arnhem*. If any
of these three Posts had been lost, yet it could not have

happen'd without good Conditions, and so retiring the men to strengthen either the more inward Garisons, or the main Camp, which would have laen ready to defend the Passes of their Rivers. And if at the worst, they had fail'd in this, yet the *French* Army must afterwards, either have attacqued a fortifi'd Camp of Twenty thousand men, or left such an Army behind them, when they marcht towards *Utrecht*, and into the heart of the Provinces; Both of which would have been Attempts, that, I think, have hardly been enterprised with success upon any Invasion.

There seems at least some appearance of Order and Conduct in this Scheme of Defence; Whereas there was none, in theirs: But perhaps the greatness of the Tempest from abroad, and of the Factions at home, either broke the heart, or distracted the course, of their Counsels. And besides, such old Sea-men in so strong a Ship, that had weathered so many Storms without loss, could not but think it hard, to throw over-board so much of their Lading before This began. After all, I know very well, That nothing is so hard, as to give wise Counsel before Events; and nothing so easie, as, after them, to make wise Reflections. Many things seem true in Reason, and prove false in Experience: Many, that are weakly consulted, are executed with Success. Therefore, to conclude, We must all acknowledg, That wisdom and Happiness dwell with God alone; And, among mortal men, (both of their Persons and their States,) Those are the wisest, that commit the fewest Follies; and those the happiest, that meet with the fewest Misfortunes.

FINIS

www.ingramcontent.com/pod-product-compliance
Ingram Content Group UK Ltd.
Pitfield, Milton Keynes, MK11 3LW, UK
UKHW042144280225
455719UK00001B/75